The earth culture music rainbow

By Abraham ghasemi

Copyright © 2018 Abraham ghasemi

All rights reserved. No part of this book may be reproduced in any form or by any electronic or mechanical means, including information storage and retrieval systems, without permission in writing from the publisher, except by reviewers, who may quote brief passages in a review. All the intellectual ideas, innovations, inventions and teaching methods in this book, are absolute to the author. Making any software or VST with systems of this book, without the author's permission is limited. The author has embedded all the tables and diagrams, illustrations, photographs, and their digital design.

cover illustration by Ali khiabanian © 2018

ISBN: 978-1942912439
Published by Supreme Art, Reseda, CA, USA
Library of Congress Control Number: 2018965470

Visit: aphiloarts@gmail.com

Dedication

Dedicated to the king of heaven, the Creator of the universe and the king of affection. Thanks and appreciation of the loved ones who support me in this six years of writing this project. My mom and dad, and my Dear Music Master Haleh Soltanmohammadi that she taught me the basic lessons of music. Moreover, she showed me the frequencies of affection.

Contents

The earth culture music rainbow.

Dedication 3
Preface 6
Introduction 8

Chapter I The wonders of the world of sound .. 12

The language of the universe 14
The wonder of nature 15
The highest perfection of humanity 17
The immortal energy of Existence 19
Originality of music 20
Transparency of music 21
Introduction to Sound 22
About octave 24
Intervals 25
Chords 26
Figured bass 27
Scale or mode 27
Keys 28

Circle of fifths..28

Timing 30

Dynamics 30

Rhythm 31

Ear Training Exercises...35

Chord Component intervals 43

Persian chords..45

Chapter II Guitar as the brain of music..........47

The brain of music 48

Sequence numbers 50

Full fretboard notes diagram and equivalent frets 54

Diagrams study guide..55

  Basic **positions for right-hands**........................ 56

  Basic positions **for left-hands**........................ 68

The pick ring...80

Chapter III Special perfection for guitarists .. 81

Professional modes and scales 82

  Professional modes and scales for right-hands ... 86

  Professional modes and scales for left-hands 108

Chapter IV The world music pyramid..........131

How the pyramid works.....................................132

Preface

Hello friends and loved ones, Greetings to all artists and art lovers. I am Abraham, A young artist and a lover of peace, love, and hope. Music is the voice of the lord, the creator of the universe. Music is the language of the universe, the language of love and hope. My artistic name is philoarts, its Means interested in the arts.

Since I was a child, I was thinking about music every day. I listened to the sounds of nature, and I am so excited about the wonders of the universe. In my childhood I perceived my existence in the universe, I understood that I could understand the order of the universe, And I realized that I could give orders in this world, based on the principles and rules of the universe. So I can do creativity.

I have always been in my mind. Moreover, all my childhood, to understand the phenomena of being and physics passed. The sounds of nature and creatures and humans and even engines, it was enough to understand everything, understand Being or not being of phenomena, Personality and behavior of the sensations, Emotions, and modes of phenomena.

I could understand, everyone and everything in their sound frequencies, and melodies. I have been learning music from science and nature. The electronic guitar had all the functionality for Production of sounds. I accepted this instrument as my friend, and I have lived with it. In the future, you will hear the music like the sound of a heartbeat. Love starts, and love has no end.

Introduction

This book is a revelation for all musicians. Moreover, it will change your mind about the guitar and world music. Of course, the guitar is the brain of music an instrument with the ability of emergency. I chose the guitar as my instrument, and in this book, I will introduce you a new language of music, the guitar's language. Dictionary of Guitar and the Applied Music Theory for Guitarists and other musicians, Beginner, Advanced, professional and super professional. For right-handed and left-handed guitarists with a visual and practical mental learning method; Subjective classification of content. With this language, you will able to understand everything about music; all secrets, all the world music and the guitar positions in your mind as well as A real shard guitarist, and finally as well as the brain of music, you can learn the cultures of the United Nations from around the world, like the music rainbow. other musicians, pianists, composers and music teachers, also can use this book as a new way of learning or creating music. So learning and mastering the table and procedures that I have created and planned, is essential for Understanding. Music theory is so important for someone who wants to understand music and learn this musical language.

This book contains four chapters. The first chapter gives a brief explanation of the concept of music and philosophy. Short music theory and up to daily ear training schedule will continue.

The Second chapter; (guitar as the brain of music), reveals all the secrets of the guitar. You may have read many guitar books. However, you will find perfection and evolution in this chapter. All the positions are classified on the guitar fretboard, the intervals on the guitar, basic chords positions, basic scales, and modes positions, figured bass and advanced chords positions. In picking styles, fingering styles and tapping styles, you can use your techniques and styles. When you be master in the second chapter, you will be a guitar shared. Just with your ease, ears and your mind, with the simplest possible way.

Chapter third Includes 12 geographical music modes, from the all over the world for the guitar. These 12 modes came out of the world music pyramid, (World Music Pyramid is in chapter 4) and these 12 modes are very close together. These modes have a longitudinal and transverse relationship, And the modes are from 12 geographic locations of the earth, With different cultures — different peoples, different races, 12 modes from the west and east of the earth. These 12 modes are harnessed and positioned for guitar. The tables are learnable. This chapter automatically teaches you the method of positioning modes on the guitar fretboard, From one octave to two octaves and multi octaves.

In the fourth chapter; You will become familiar with the world music pyramid, my innovative system for creating music. Longitudinal and transverse combination of all world music modes. The world modes, and scales of all people. Moreover, relatives and the races of the earth. All their scales and modes of the scales, Connections of modes and harmonies Like a chain in a functional table. It works in different ways to create multi-tonal and my innovative system parallel-tonal Compositions. It is with Special and traditional Harmonization. The pyramid consists of two faces Page on the left side is Pyramid, the place of the World Music Modes. Moreover, the Page on the right side is the Prism.it is Harmonization for the modes. Harmonies have longitudinal and transverse relationships. Everything about humanity and world music is in this chapter.

Finally, there are 15 Persians modes, that I had to develop them from traditional Persian music, with Combining 4 Tetrachords of Persian Music. Moreover, by analysis the 12th Maqams of the ancient and ethnic music of Iran. I designed these 15 modes Persian modes are close to the world music and have scattered connections. Persian music simplification and clarification for all the musicians of the world, they can be understood and Performing. I also devised Persian chords to harmonize these Persian modes. For all the years of my life, I have to understand the relationship between traditional music nations and connect cultures.

CHAPTER I
THE WONDERS OF THE WORLD OF SOUND

In the beginning, there was nothing but pure solitary vibrations traveling through the air. That happened to hit our ears in a way that inspired us to assign them numerical values. After them came the vibrations in between them. They went to the balance between the amounts of time between the frequencies which we call rhythm. We decided that some frequencies sound good with others and called that harmony. All of these notes could be combined and organized into melody rhythm and harmony in any way we wanted. However, what about this phenomenon has spanned millennia? What about these combinations of frequencies and the space in between them have shaped cultures bridge Geographic and linguistic boundaries and brought nations to their knees?

Why is music so powerful? Some try to answer this question with neuroscience, some attempt an anthropological or evolutionary viewpoint. However, I do not think anyone can fully answer this question Until they look into the eyes of another human being When they light up with the sound of a note. The eyes they say are the visual gateway into another human soul. Moreover, without souls, each note is simply a vibrational quiver into the cold.

Could it be that we are merely organic disposable inconsequential clumps of tissue? There has got to be something bigger than ourselves that we were never made to understand possibly, these are the combinations of vibrations that hold us together when the rest of the world seems to be falling apart.

the language of the universe

Music is the language of the universe. This is a deeper understanding around. The universe is a part of a music sheet. What dose frequencies and harmonizes mean? What is the revelation between people's lives and the nature Composing? What human's dreams mean? We are another symbol of the universe; we are another reflection of the universe. The frequency of the universe is music. Everything in the universe connects with music. Music is a reality of the unique aspect of the expression of the being. We get to hear the music of natural phenomena. Finally, we are feeling the beauty of Sounds Source, the beauty of Physical rules that the Music reveals the elegance of physical rules. In a different vibrational energetic expression, we get to see ourselves in each other; we get to see ourselves in nature. We are the whole having the experience of being, an individual that is ultimately reconnecting with the whole.

The wonder of nature

Take a look at the scenery of nature. Touch the stars of the sky, Movement of winds, Water Currents. Imagine your favorite nature in your mind. Are natural phenomena not regular and coherent? Do not have harmony? Music is one of the secrets of creation and existence. Knowing the music can be got the wonder of nature. The glory of the human is the loving the Wisdom. Roles of music are every verse in nature? Yes is it so close the physics, but I am talking about something more than physics. Every phenomenon in nature has an orchestral. It is so amazing that we can understand it; We can fill it and Detect music from every drop of the universe. Why is enlightenment in human concrete? We are thinking, and we are aware, we are miracles, we are more than one object in the material environment. We are seeing the universe, is this world depends on being ours. We understand the world around us. Moreover, understanding for us is a feeling.

When we see the stars in the sky, or when we look at the physical formulas, or when we recognize different patterns; The secrets and wonders of the universe are not a mystery. However, it is food for our intelligence and medicine for our wounds. The universe is full of simple and complex patterns. These patterns are simply revealed to our minds, like methods of understanding and receiving music, Like music sheets. The whole universe is a musical sheet. Wherever we look, music is written in nature, playing them is our art. Music is a cosmetic extract for our thirsty minds to understand. All secrets are analyzed with music. How is the flower of fiery love restless? Have you blossomed for music? Look at the stars, see the patterns and understand their notes, then play music sheet of stars, then kiss the universe peacefully, and Kiss the earth with your steps, love nature as the energy you are. Flay in the cosmos of love, swim in the waters of life, Be Gracious like the lush plains of Generosity. After the winter eventually springs, the flowers will blossom. Swim in the oceans of Kindness Whit dolphins, and loves creations and creations in the earth.

A close look at the Creatures, they are undermining way they are alive. They know what should do in the universe, in nature each animal created in Purpose each one of them has different goals, and try to do it well in all life. What is the difference between humans and other Creatures? The way we are intelligent Creatures, and we have to understand and chose the best way in life?

The highest perfection of humanity

When we have to get the best experience in the universe? When will we find the highest humankind civilization? Where is the highest level of menology? Each one of us has a mind and one soul. The secret is, the mind and heart and soul works to gather, to be a human in The highest perfection of humanity; Not in the roles, Not in clothes, Not in social positions, Not in religious law and mystical tricks. Only and only in the heart, Within the human itself, The free mind and clean soul and transparent life. This is the way of salvation humanity. So that salvation just comes with harmony with other humans, nature, and creatures, as well as the music is. The soul the heart and the mind working to gather in music. This is a deceptive an order, and music is the language of love, that every human should learn how to analyze music haw to hear music, and have music in self and finally create music. For that person, everything is wonderful and felling the love of creator in the phenomenon of creation and nature. Let start love everything, in every breath and walking, in the light of pace, in every heart bits of love, and hopes forever be a perfect human for this wonderful world.

Music helps you to understand the universe is always Companion with you. Creator has always been Companion for you, you have always been a part of the Creator, and you will continue always to be a part of the Creator. Music is the language of the universe. We can feel it sound travels. Moreover, waves touch and reach everything in the universe, including our souls, to be in touch with this music. Humanity has just chosen to have the illusion of separation into individual expression, which looks like an individuality. You have a unique individual vibration that only you carry, much like the snowflake. There are billions of snowflakes, and they all from a perspective of a species look the same. However, when you get into each one, they all have a unique signature, just as you do. Every atom, every organism are made of energy. Without energy, there are no vibrations we all have different energy patterns. Each one of us has a unique interaction with every piece of music.

The immortal energy of Existence

In the universe, Love energy Keep the structures together. Love is the immortal energy of Existence. The relationship between the cells of each organ is love. Also, Organisms play the music of Life together. If the cells of an organ, do not make love music together; In the organ, Cancer cells will be created. The relationship between cells is not a dictatorship. Love is on Between each cell with another cell, and its purpose is to play the music of life. Love is the secret of living in a community. Music is based on love. Lover and beloved are united in love. They will be the Composers of Love Orchestral and have a common goal; making the love of life, Until the end of life. Like the cells of an organ. They are in everything Common and have the same Tastes, values, and beliefs. In music Structure and harmony is visible This is the same love, music love is the immortal energy of Existence,

Anyone has dived into the realm of love. In a broad way to real music lovers, there is freedom there, and there is trust there. The rhythm of your heart beats and organs all is found in all sound effects. What emotions? Your body is interacting with these sound waves. Love thyself to see thyself have self-actualization. So we are starting to awaken into the music of freedom and joy. Love emotions that we are, great gratitude for the glory of the god and this creation, love is the Companion of all frequencies and all emotions, so when you embody love which is who you are. You will feel this harmony of nature. They all communicate on the vibrational frequency.

Originality of music

The human body is very wonderful; Music has a wonderful effect on human physical health and psyche health. The nervous system controls the body's vital system; Your favorite music influences the vital mode of your body. From ancient times to known, many tribal nations used music therapy. Thoughts are transmitted with poems, and feelings are transmitted with music. Music character is Like water. When poetry and music are combined; In fact, music is used as an effect to transmit the poet's feelings. So in this case, music is part of the poem. The main form of the artwork is poetry and literature, Not a musical work. Music tells something else. In my opinion, there is music therapy in music without poetry — moreover, poetry that is emotionally sad in not good to make lyric music. It is not suitable for lyric music production. That is why may cause depression in the audience. Feet a man a fish, you feed them for the day. However, teach a man haw to fish, you feed him for a lifetime. Let's start playing with the depths of heart and make a good relationship with music. Also, thinking to the universe everywhere. The material becomes the energy, and the energy becomes the material. The result of moving active energy in the material environment is Frequency. Moreover, vibration is a phenomenon of activating energy between the energy. Also, matter encounter Sunlight has mass and frequency, and the sound is the result of energy transfer between the material molecules.

Transparency of music

Music is the share of all cultures and races. It is not the only music that is the heritage of humanity. It is clear to the clarity of the water, and white as well as the whiteness of the snow. Without oppression, without ignorance without racism, without violence, without falsehood. Music is a spirituality, a pure spirituality, a love of the world of truth. Music is the voice of God. The musician is a human with a commitment to ethics, Humanitarians, a soldier of the peace army. People of the earth have different beliefs, different religions, Different cultures, various languages Different races. With all these differences, Music is a partnership of people around the world. Art is the cultural contribution of the world, and in music, we are all one. In music, all the people of the world are a civilization. And finally, music is the set of regular and harmonious sounds that have a definite goal. Bees drink nectar from flowers and produce honey. Moreover, humans learn science and physics and produce music.

Introduction to Sound

Five different main aspects can define the sound. The first aspect of sound is pitch. Pitch is also called the frequency. Sound it also has a dynamic it also called the amplitude of the sound. Timber is the tone color of a sound. The envelope of the sound can define articulation. Finally, the last aspect of sound is duration. The sine wave is the purest and simplest form of sound, and it is not found in nature. However, it is helpful when it comes down to explaining frequencies When sine wave oscillates three-hundred and sixty degrees and makes a completed cycle that is a full cycle. The amount of completed cycles that fit in one second is the frequency. Frequency is also called the Pitch. Pitch is defined as the distance between sound waves, in a sound that you might hear. If you hear a sound that has a high pitch, that note when viewed as a waveform has waves that are very close together, the distance between the waves are short, and therefore, the pitch is high. A pitch that sounds low has a very long wavelength. The distance between these wavelengths are very long, and therefore, the pitch is very low. So the distance between the waves is what determines the pitch of a sound. Higher frequencies can go up that twenty thousand completed cycles per second or twenty thousand hertz, which we call 20 kilohertz. We can divide our groups of frequencies directly into two groups: low frequencies and high frequencies. Low frequencies are called bass, and high frequencies are called

Treble. The frequency range of the human ear ranges from twenty Hertz up to twenty kilohertz. We do lose some of our hearing capabilities when we get older, that is why older people cannot hear higher frequencies. Musical sounds have a certain frequency, like a flute. However, Non-musical sounds do not have a certain frequency, like an explosion. Pure sine wave sandy cannot be found in nature. However, all sounds that are found in nature like speech or any music related sounds is a composition of various sine waves at different amplitudes. A concert "A" is tuned at 440 Hertz. If we play that A-note on a guitar or a piano it is the same note, but still we can hear that it is a piano or a guitar. That is because the fundamental frequency is 440 Hertz but the harmonics determine the character of an instrument. The harmonics make up the 'Timbre,' or the character of the sound. Timbre is an interesting term it refers to the color of the sound; the color of a sound refers to the qualities of the tone that you are hearing. Some terms that might be thrown around in music would be something like Reedy, brassy, warm, biting and sharp or mellow, terms like these help musicians to describe the way that a note should sound. Regarding the overall quality of the notes and that is what Timbre is. Reasons for influencing the Different Timbres for a guitar or a piano. It can be The shape of the instrument, the way that the notes are being generated, like if they are fingerpicked, or if they are, well, hit with hammers, and that all determine the way that it sounds. So the material in the instrument is being made out of, and even the type of wood can influence the way that it sounds. The envelope of the sound defines the articulation of sound. Volume is over time. All musical notes begin with a sharp attack, followed by a short decay, after that the note sustained over whatever period the duration dictates. Moreover, then the note is released and it decays over time until the sound disappears. The attack, the decay, the sustain, and the release that is the articulation of sound. The duration of sound is kind of an obvious one it is the total length of the sound or the notes in the case of music. Duration is represented by the full length not just sustain of the note the attack, the decay, and the reliefs are also parts of the duration of the note. Dynamics define how loud or how soft a sound is when you look at a sound with a loud dynamic. You will see a very tall waveform. Because these waves are very high, very tall, the sound is loud it has a large amplitude. A softer sound will have a shorter amplitude. When the amplitude is shorter, the sound is softer. So again when looking at dynamics, the height of the waves determines the dynamic of the sound.

About octave

Octave is a perfect distance between 2 Pitches. In each octave, the notes are repeated. Moreover, Sound frequency doubles with each octave. Each octave is divided into 12 equal parts. It makes 12 music notes. Each octave includes 12 tones and tones repeat themselves in other octaves. There are 10 octaves from 20Hz to 20kHz. The smallest interval between two notes is a semitone. There are 12 semitones in an octave these would be the chromatic steps. There are 100 cents in every semitone. 50 cents sharp or flat would be exactly halfway in between two semitones. Often when singers are slightly sharp or flat, they are in the range of about 15 percent or 15 cents from the actual pitch. Choir singers try to keep their vibrato narrow to about 10 cents in both directions whereas some singers have a much wider vibrato where the pitch might oscillate as much or more than a semitone.

Intervals

What are intervals? An interval is a distance between two pitches. There are two types of intervals. The first is two notes played simultaneously, known as a harmonic interval. The second is two notes played separately, known as a melodic interval. There are 12 intervals in western music, have vastly different sound characteristics. There are Two properties describe intervals; The first being the quality: perfect, major, minor, augmented, diminished, and the second is the number: unison, second, third, fourth, fifth, sixth, seventh, eighth, eleventh, thirteen. The number intervals can become diminished or augmented but never perfect. Intervals are the Base and foundation of polyphonic music. Interval recognition is so essential for ear training.

Chords

Chords made of combination Intervals. The basic chords are triads. The first thing is that a triad is made up of three different notes. We can have chords with four notes, five notes, six notes, seven notes, all sorts of different combinations. However, for a chord to be a triad, there have to be three notes in the chord. Another quality of a triad is that; its pitches can be arranged in stacked thirds. A Tertian is a chord that's built up of stacked thirds. Each of the three notes in the Triad has a particular name When we stack a triad in thirds. The bottom note is the root, and the middle is the third above the root, and so the top note is going to be called the fifth. We have only 4 type of triads. In music Major triad, minor triad, augmented tread, diminished triad. Also, Sus2 and sus4 chords have three notes, but they are not going to be called triads. By adding more intervals to the triads and three notes Chords. We can have multi-note chords, with four notes, five notes, six notes, seven notes.

Triads

	Root	3rd	5th	Symbols
Major	P1	M3	P5	M
Minor	P1	m3	P5	m
Augmented	P1	M3	A5	+
Diminished	P1	m3	D5	o

Figured bass

Fundamental of the figured bass. The figured bass is a system of representing chords and their inversions, instead of the combination of Roman numerals and letters. The Roman number details the Chord in which degree of the scale is? That is called Chord Function. And the letter shows the inversion. A triad Chord in root position called five three, well because the notes in the chord are a 3rd and a fifth above the root. Five three is just another way of saying root position. When the third of the triad chord is in the base, this means the chord is in the first inversion, the numbers six three. Fifth note of the chord is in the base we decide to use figured base six four, represents the second inversion. Root this is just a small step into figured bass to represent inversions.

Scale or mode

The scale is a chain of notes in an octave. Scale notes are ordered in the state of ascending descending. Each scale has degrees and degrees are written with Roman numerals (I, II, III, IV, V, VI, VII, VIII, IX, X, XI, XII ...). Degrees refers to the position of a particular note on a scale relative to the tonic. Moreover, mode created from each degree of the scale, in each degree of a scale or mode we can have harmonized chords, intervals that can be there. Chord Function Specifies the position of the Chords in Scale and also specifies the harmonic Relationship of the chords with the other chords in the scale.

Keys

Scales can put up in every tone of the music. Clearer explains: there is 12 pitch class in one octave, and we can play a scale in each note of 12 notes of music. Each scale has modes that come from the scale s notes degrees .one basic example. If you lock at the white keys on the piano, there are seven notes in a heptatonic scale. Each digresses of the scale is a mode. C Ionian mode is the major scale, D Dorian, E Phrygian, F Lydian, G Mixolydian, A Aeolian mode know as minor and finally B locran this is a case and can transpose to another key of the 12 pianos keys. Each key has a different filing and pitch will change in any keys Aeolian minor, and Ionian major in the cercal of fifth Are neighbors, and they are Relative to Together.

Moreover, other modes are in degrees of this scales. Key signatures Indicate, which notes at each pitch will change. Then just by changing the key signature of a music sheet it will by transpose to another key.

Circle of fifths

Circle of fifths shows the relationships among the 12 pitch classes: Key signatures, and the associated major and minor keys.

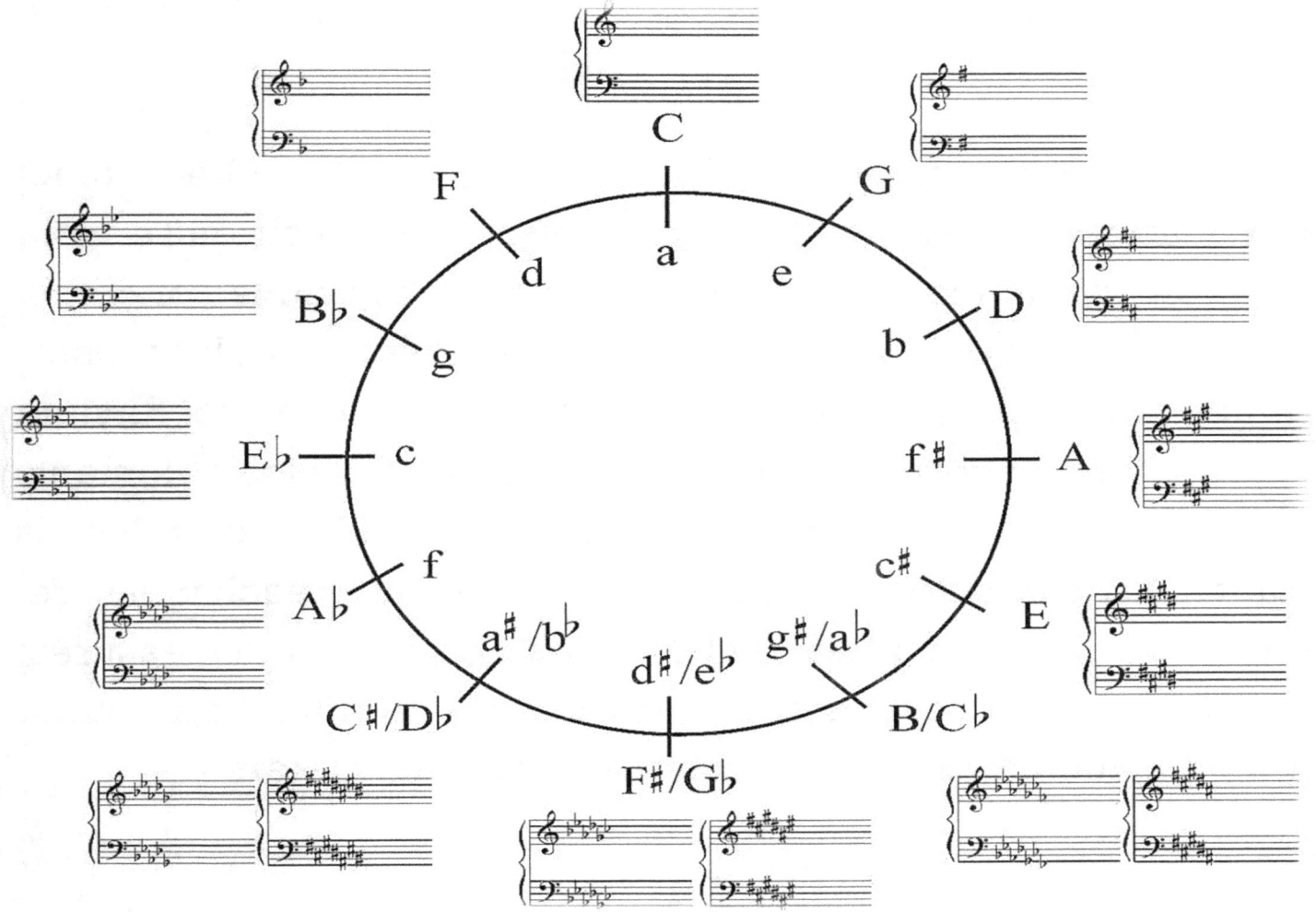

Major key	Minor key	Key signature	Major key	Minor key	Key signature
C M	A m		C M	A m	
G M	E m	F#	F M	D m	B♭
D M	B m	F#,C#	B♭ M	G m	B♭,E♭
A M	F# m	F#,C#,G#	E♭ M	C m	B♭,E♭,A♭
E M	C# m	F#,C#,G#,D#	A♭ M	F m	B♭,E♭,A♭,D♭
B M	G# m	F#,C#,G#,D#,A#	D♭ M	B♭ m	B♭,E♭,A♭,D♭,G♭
F# M	D# m	F#,C#,G#,D#,A#,E#	G♭ M	E♭ m	B♭,E♭,A♭,D♭,G♭,C♭
C# M	A# m	F#,C#,G#,D#,A#,E#,B#	C♭ M	A♭ m	B♭,E♭,A♭,D♭,G♭,C♭,F♭

Timing

Time is the existence. Timing is the ability to keep time, and understanding rhythm accurately, and synchronize note duration with the beat. So tempo in divisions of time. Metronome is a device for dividing the time into regular pulses. Tempo is the specified Speed for play a piece of music. Rhythm is a repeated pattern and sequence of strong and weak elements in time. Measure signature Specifies which note value is equivalent to one beat and how many beats are in each measure, and where the Strong Beat and the Weak Beat is in the measures. There are various types of time signatures, simple, compound, complex, mixed, additive, fractional, irrational meters.

Dynamics

Dynamics is the variation in loudness between notes or phrases of a music piece. Dynamics is very important in music performance, and also in composing and Music Recording. Dynamics is the final element of transfer feelings of music pieces.

Name	Level	Letters	Name	Level	Letters
mezzo-piano		mp	mezzo-forte	average	mf
piano	soft	p	forte	loud	f
pianissimo	softer	pp	fortissimo	louder	ff
pianississimo	very soft	ppp	fortississimo	very loud	fff

Rhythm

On the next page, you will see the Note value table. In Contain Basic rhythm patterns table is a great way to improve your rhythmic filling. Just use your head for filling the Rhythm, and for each Metronome pulse head down and for Decide Metronome pulse to 2 parts juts head up. Moreover, gate starts reading Rhythm Patterns with Letter (da). Close your eyes Read each rhythmic pattern in your mind and save it into your heart. After repeated exercises, you will recognize these rhythms in music, and you will perform them in improvisation. Then your Rhythmic Dictation will be professional, Also, the third table of this section Tempo and measures. This table contains the patterns for Regular exercise, Tempo, Measure signature, and Bars. According to this program for each pattern Practice 5 minutes.

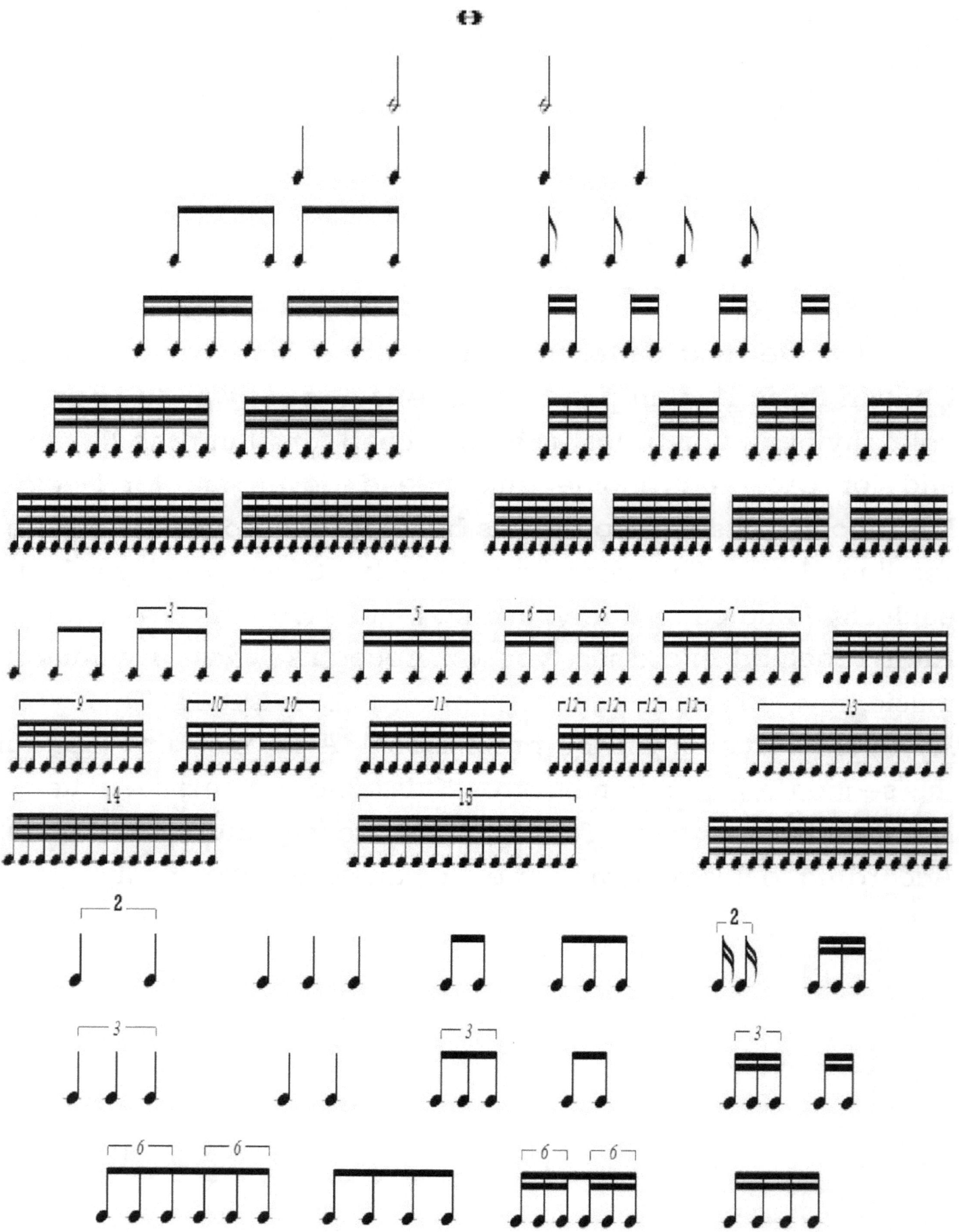

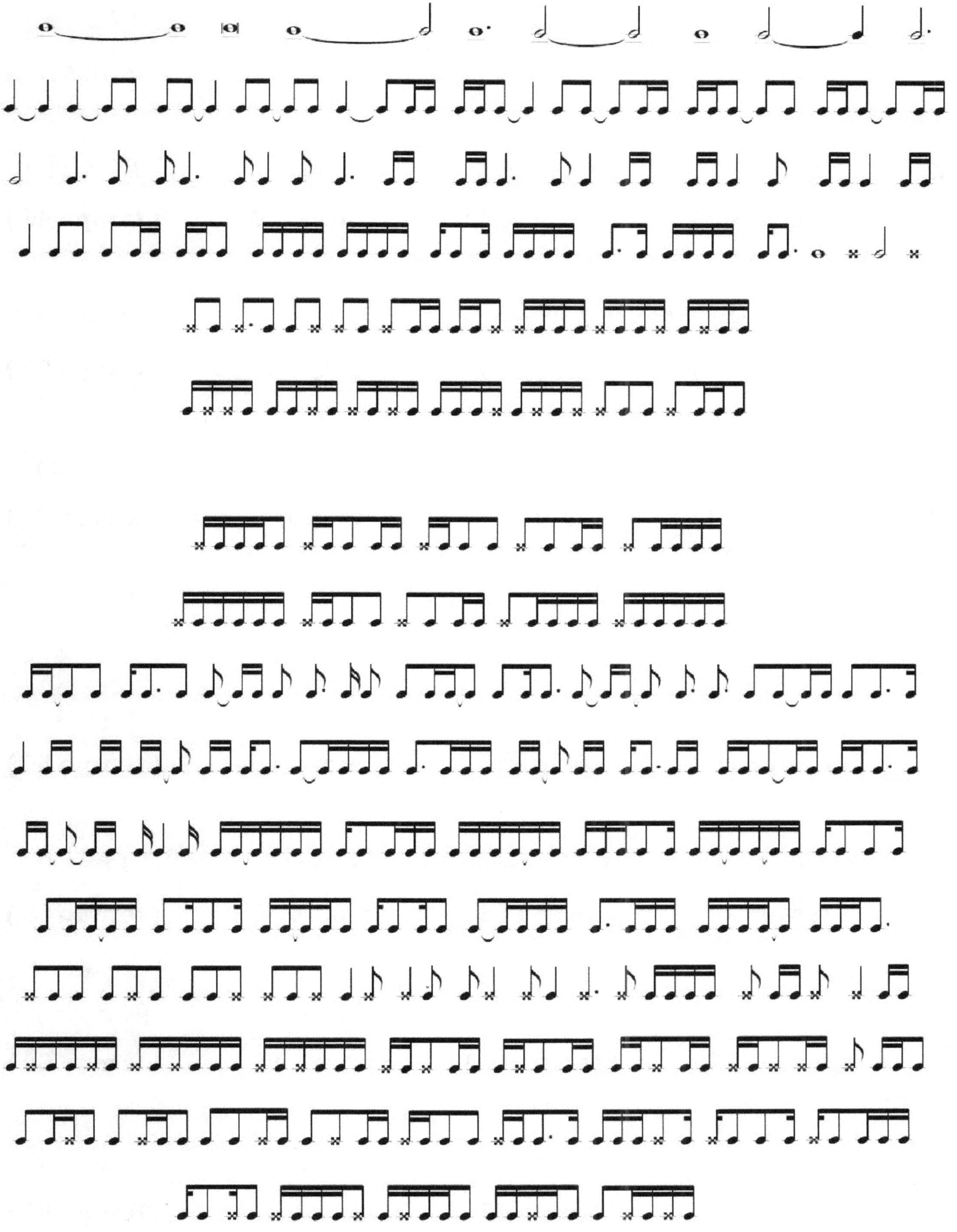

1/4	(1 bar) (tempo 55)	(2 bars) (tempo 50)	(3 bars) (tempo 45)	(4 bars) (tempo 40)
2/4	(1 bar) (tempo 60)	(2 bars) (tempo 55)	(3 bars) (tempo 50)	(4 bars) (tempo 45)
3/4	(1 bar) (tempo 65)	(2 bars) (tempo 60)	(3 bars) (tempo 55)	(4 bars) (tempo 50)
4/4	(1 bar) (tempo 70)	(2 bars) (tempo 65)	(3 bars) (tempo 60)	(4 bars) (tempo 55)
3/8	(1 bar) (tempo 65)	(2 bars) (tempo 60)	(3 bars) (tempo 55)	(4 bars) (tempo 50)
6/8	(1 bar) (tempo 70)	(2 bars) (tempo 65)	(3 bars) (tempo 60)	(4 bars) (tempo 55)
9/8	(1 bar) (tempo 75)	(2 bars) (tempo 70)	(3 bars) (tempo 65)	(4 bars) (tempo 60)
12/8	(1 bar) (tempo 80)	(2 bars) (tempo 75)	(3 bars) (tempo 70)	(4 bars) (tempo 65)

Ear Training Exercises

Exercise; Open your jaw, Tongue down your teeth, close your lips and close your eyes and sing in your head OOM, and enhancing your voice, if you do it right, you will feel the vibration in your head, like the sound of an engine. That Vibration is the frequency of intensifies in your head. in your inner ear; you hear the frequency of your head. Your throat is the same frequency Relax and remembers this shake. Free up your voice. Widen your comfortable range. Improve your vocal pitch control. Hone your sense of tuning. Train your ear for semitones and tones.

Exercise 1: if you have a piano hold sustain pedal. And play one tone and all its octaves tones randomly in rhythm, and sing OOO. fell the vibration of the tone. And tray to memories the tone character. Tray this for every 12 notes of music. Imagine below table is a train of 12 carriages. Per carriage respectively is a pitch class. Repeat this practice in this series; this will train your ears at all tones. Accurate Sense of Pitch. With this exercise.

TONES

Exercise 2: The table below shows how to read the next page. This is about ascending and descending intervals from the chromatic scale, that placed on the middle line. In this exercise from each note of the chromatic scale, read the ascending and descending intervals.

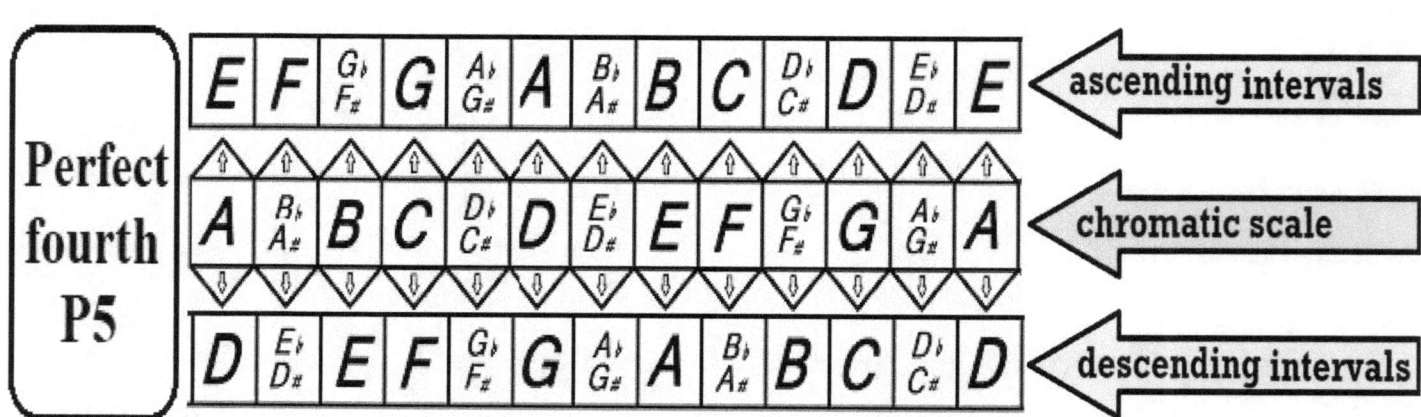

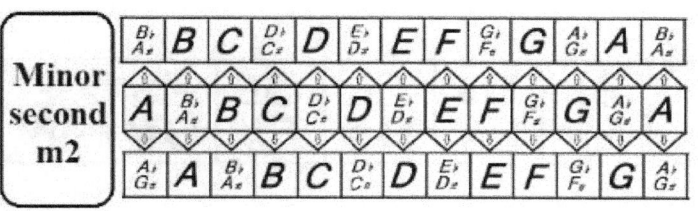
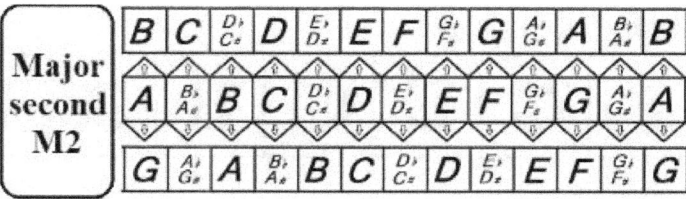
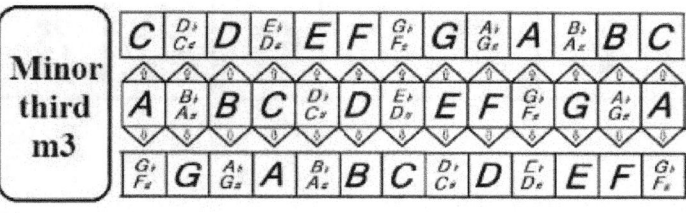
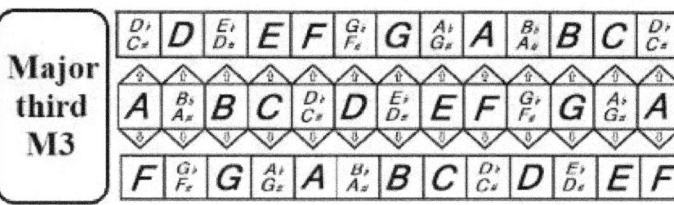
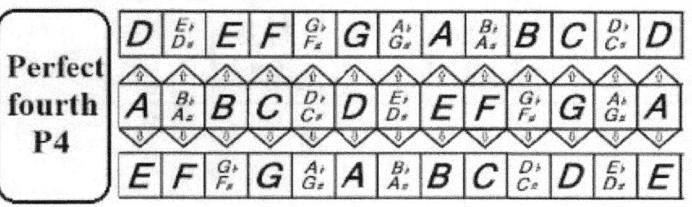
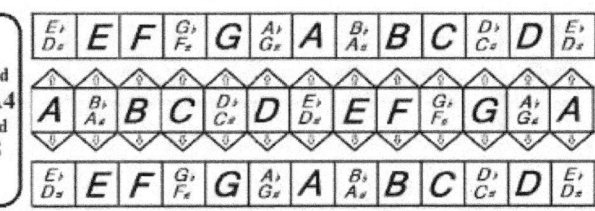
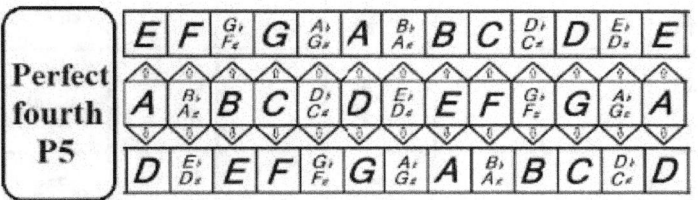
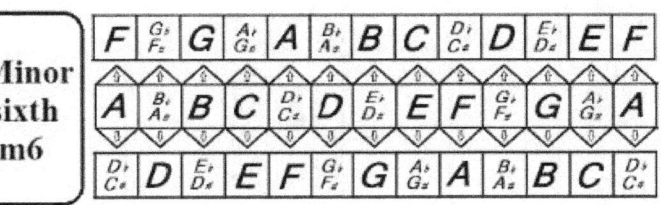
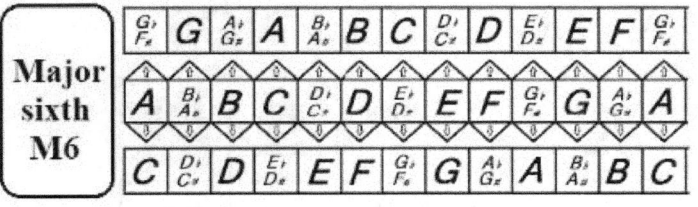
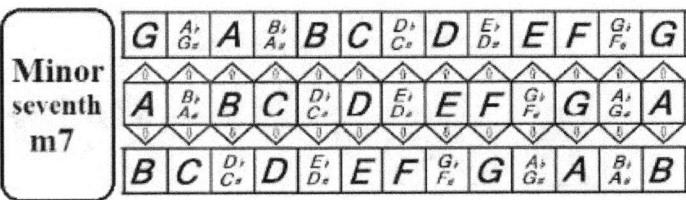
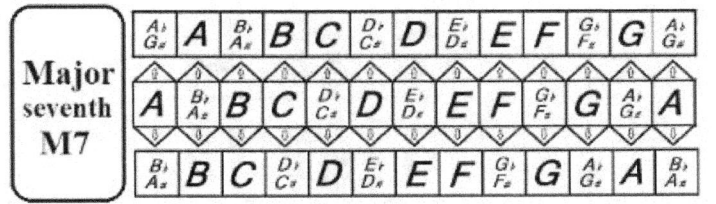

TONES

A	C	E	G	B	D	F	Bb/A#	Db/C#	Eb/D#	Gb/F#	Ab/G#	A

CHROMATIC

A	Bb/A#	B	C	Db/C#	D	Eb/D#	E	F	Gb/F#	G	Ab/G#	A

HEXATONIC

A	B	Db/C#	Eb/D#	F	G	A
C	D	E	Gb/F#	Ab/G#	Bb/A#	C

ALL POSSIBLE DIMINISHED ARPEGGIOS

A		C		Eb/D#		Gb/F#		A
D		F		Ab/G#		B		D
G		Bb/A#		Db/C#		E		G

ALL POSSIBLE AUGMENTED ARPEGGIOS

A	Db/C#	F
C	E	Ab/G#
D	Gb/F#	Bb/A#
G	B	Eb/D#

Db/C#	F	A
E	Ab/G#	C
Gb/F#	Bb/A#	D
B	Eb/D#	G

F	A	Db/C#
Ab/G#	C	E
Bb/A#	D	Gb/F#
Eb/D#	G	B

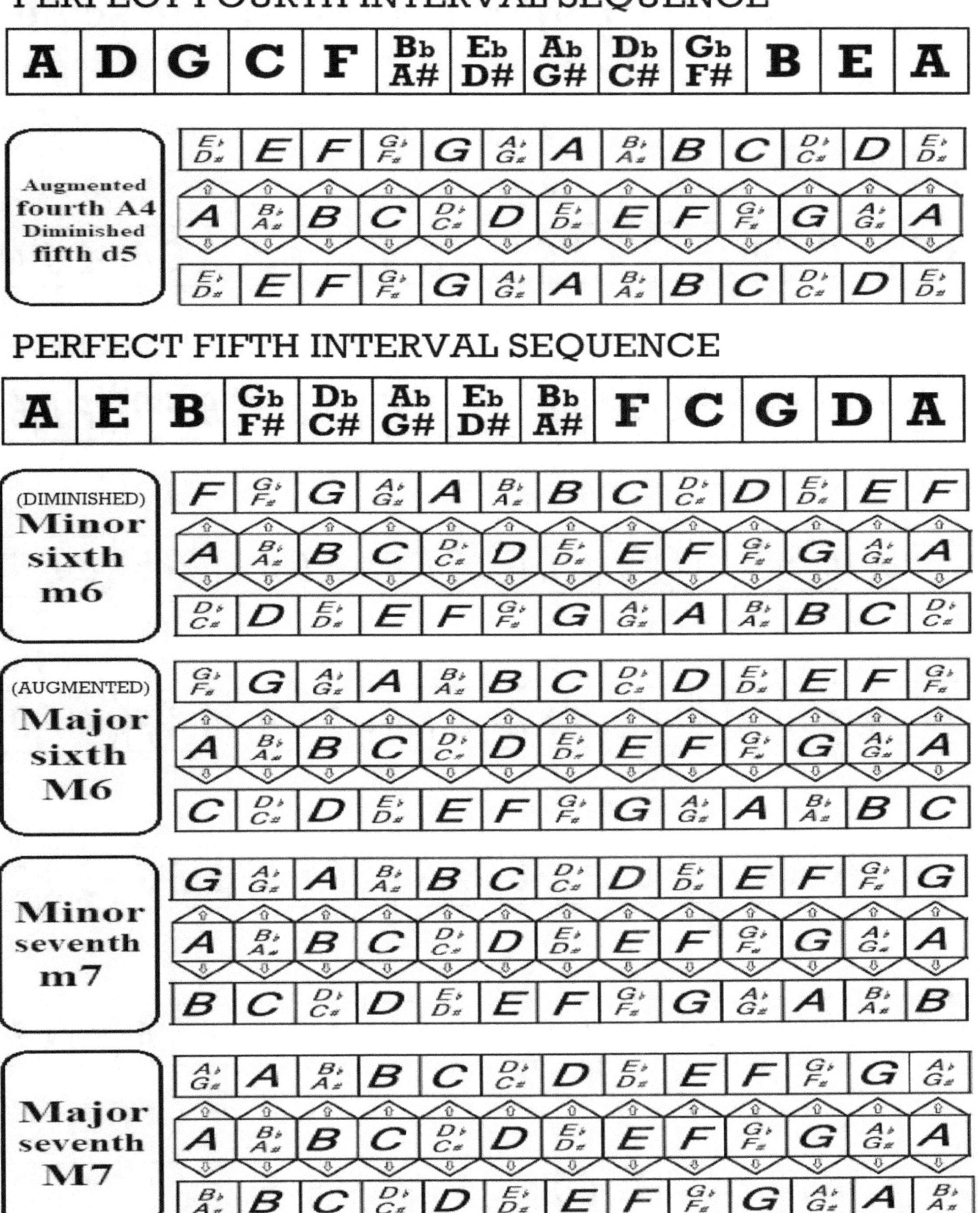

figured bass arpegios of the diatonic scale

| 5 3 | 6 3 | 6 4 | 5 3 | 5 3 | 6 3 | 6 4 | 5 3 |

ACE ⇨ CEA ⇨ EAC ⇨ ACE ⇨ ECA ⇨ CAE ⇨ AEC ⇨ ECA

BDF ⇨ DFB ⇨ FBD ⇨ BDF ⇨ FDB ⇨ DBF ⇨ BFD ⇨ FDB

CEG ⇨ EGC ⇨ GCE ⇨ CEG ⇨ GEC ⇨ ECG ⇨ CGE ⇨ GEC

DFA ⇨ FAD ⇨ ADF ⇨ DFA ⇨ AFD ⇨ FDA ⇨ DAF ⇨ AFD

EGB ⇨ GBE ⇨ BEG ⇨ EGB ⇨ BGE ⇨ GEB ⇨ EBG ⇨ BGE

FAC ⇨ ACF ⇨ CFA ⇨ FAC ⇨ CAF ⇨ AFC ⇨ FCA ⇨ CAF

GBE ⇨ BEG ⇨ EGB ⇨ GBE ⇨ EBG ⇨ BGE ⇨ GEB ⇨ EBG

ALL POSSIBLE MAJOR TRIADS FIGURED BASSES

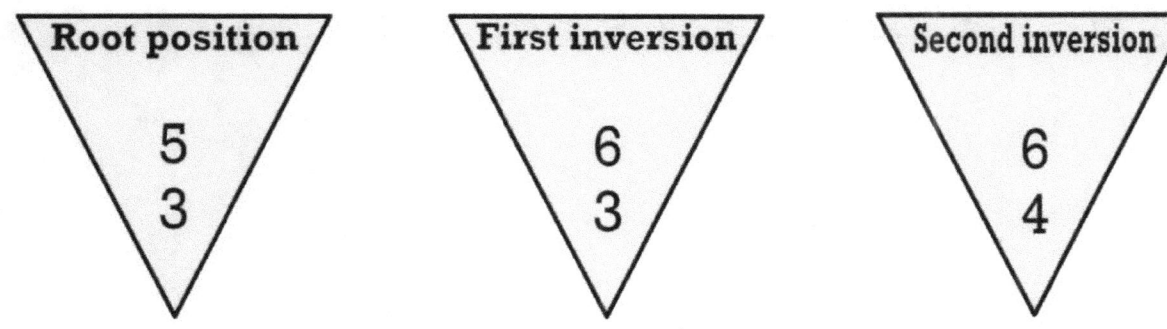

A	Db/C#	E		Db/C#	E	A		E	A	Db/C#	A
C	E	G		E	G	C		G	C	E	C
E	Ab/G#	B		Ab/G#	B	E		B	E	Ab/G#	E
G	B	D		B	D	G		D	G	B	G
B	Eb/D#	Gb/F#		Eb/D#	Gb/F#	B		Gb/F#	B	Eb/D#	B
D	Gb/F#	A		Gb/F#	A	D		A	D	Gb/F#	D
F	A	C		A	C	F		C	F	A	F
Bb/A#	D	F		D	F	Bb/A#		F	Bb/A#	D	Bb/A#
Db/C#	F	Ab/G#		F	Ab/G#	Db/C#		Ab/G#	Db/C#	F	Db/C#
Eb/D#	G	Bb/A#		G	Bb/A#	Eb/D#		Bb/A#	Eb/D#	G	Eb/D#
Gb/F#	Bb/A#	Db/C#		Bb/A#	Db/C#	Gb/F#		Db/C#	Gb/F#	Bb/A#	Gb/F#
Ab/G#	C	Eb/D#		C	Eb/D#	Ab/G#		Eb/D#	Ab/G#	C	Ab/G#

ALL POSSIBLE MINOR TRIADS FIGURED BASSES

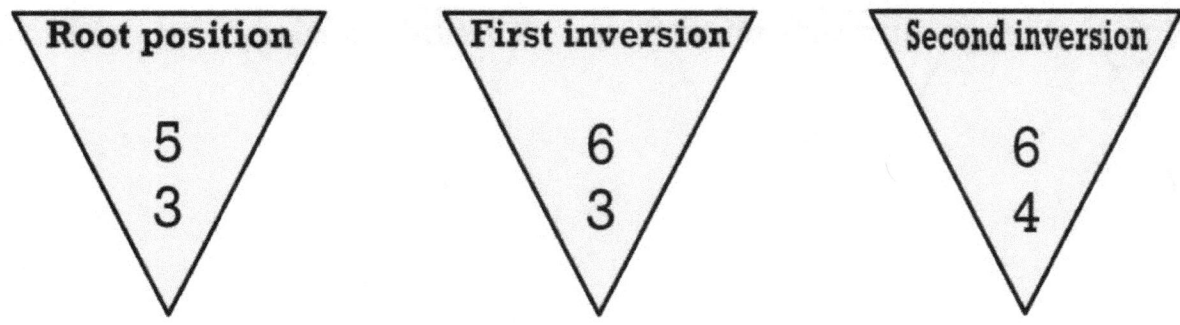

Root position	First inversion	Second inversion
5/3	6/3	6/4

A	**C**	**E**		**C**	**E**	**A**		**E**	**A**	**C**	**A**
C	Eb/D#	**G**		Eb/D#	**G**	**C**		**G**	**C**	Eb/D#	**C**
E	**G**	**B**		**G**	**B**	**E**		**B**	**E**	**G**	**E**
G	Bb/A#	**D**		Bb/A#	**D**	**G**		**D**	**G**	Bb/A#	**G**
B	**D**	Gb/F#		**D**	Gb/F#	**B**		Gb/F#	**B**	**D**	**B**
D	**F**	**A**		**F**	**A**	**D**		**A**	**D**	**F**	**D**
F	Ab/G#	**C**		Ab/G#	**C**	**F**		**C**	**F**	Ab/G#	**F**
Bb/A#	Db/C#	**F**		Db/C#	**F**	Bb/A#		**F**	Bb/A#	Db/C#	Bb/A#
Db/C#	**E**	Ab/G#		**E**	Ab/G#	Db/C#		Ab/G#	Db/C#	**E**	Db/C#
Eb/D#	Gb/F#	Bb/A#		Gb/F#	Bb/A#	Eb/D#		Bb/A#	Eb/D#	Gb/F#	Eb/D#
Gb/F#	**A**	Db/C#		**A**	Db/C#	Gb/F#		Db/C#	Gb/F#	**A**	Gb/F#
Ab/G#	**B**	Eb/D#		**B**	Eb/D#	Ab/G#		Eb/D#	Ab/G#	**B**	Ab/G#

Chord Component intervals

The note inside the brackets (x) can be deleted

MAJOR		
Chord Name	Component intervals	Symbol
Major	P1-M3-P5	M
Added Fourth	P1-M3-P4-P5	Madd4
Sixth	P1-M3-P5-M6	M6
Six Nine	P1-M3-P5-M6-M9	M6/9
Major 7th	P1-M3-P5-M7	MΔ7
Major 7	P1-M3-P5-m7	M7
Major Ninth	P1-M3-P5-M7-M9	Maj9
Major Eleventh	P1-M3-P5-M7- (9)-P11	Maj11
Major Thirteenth	P1-M3-P5-M7-(9)-(11)- M13	Maj13
Major seven sharp eleventh	P1-M3-P5-M7- #11	MΔ7#11
Major Flat Five	P1-M3-D5	Mb5

MINOR		
Chord Name	Component intervals	Symbol
Minor	P1-m3-P5	m
Minor added fourth	P1-m3-P4-P5	madd4
Minor sixth	P1-m3-P5-M6	m6
Minor seventh	P1-m3-P5-m7	m7
Minor added ninth	P1-m3-P5-M9	madd9
Minor six add nine	P1-m3-P5-M6-M9	m6/9
Minor ninth	P1-m3-P5-m7-M9	m9
Minor eleventh	P1-m3-P5-m7-(9)-P11	m11
Minor thirteenth	P1-m3-P5-m7-(9)-(11)-M13	m13
Minor/Major seventh	P1-m3-P5-M7	mΔ7
Minor/Major ninth	P1-m3-P5-M7-M9	mΔ9
Minor/Major eleventh	P1-m3-P5-M7-(9)-P11	mΔ11
Minor/Major thirteenth	P1-m3-P5-M7-(9)-(11)-M13	mΔ13
Minor seven flat fifth	P1-m3-m5-m7	m7-5 or ø

Symmetrical Chord Name	Component intervals	Symbol
Diminished	P1-m3-m5	dim (°)
Diminished Seventh	P1-m3-m5-D7	dim7 (°7)
Augmented	P1-3-M5	aug (+)

DOMINANT Chord Name	Component intervals	Symbol
Seventh	P1-M3-P5-m7	7
Ninth	P1-M3-P5-m7-M9	9
Eleventh	P1-(3)-P5-m7-(9)-P11	11
Thirteenth	P1-M3-P5-m7-(9)-(11)-M13	13
Seven sharp five	P1-M3-A5-m7	7#5
Seven flat five	P1-M3-D5-m7	7b5
Seven flat ninth	P1-M3-P5-m7-m9	7b9
Seven sharp ninth	P1-M3-P5-m7-m10	7#9
Nine sharp five	P1-M3-A5-m7-M9	9#5
Nine flat five	P1-M3-D5-m7-M9	9b5
Seven sharp five sharp nine	P1-M3-A5-m7-m10	7#5#9
Seven sharp five flat nine	P1-M3-A5-m7-m9	7#5b9
Seven flat five sharp nine	P1-M3-D5-m7-m10	7b5#9
Seven flat five flat nine	P1-M3-D5-m7-m9	7b5b9
Seven sharp eleven	P1-M3-P5-m7-M11	7#11

Persian chords

There are 15 traditional modes from the Middle East in chapter IV. Some of these mods are in the ancient maqams of Iran. Moreover, some of this modes are created from traditional music systems. I created these modes in the global system. To be understood and implemented by everyone. This 15 traditional modes Included all the music of the Eastern, Middle East.

These modes have quarter-tone intervals. A semi-tone is 100 cents, and a quarter-tone is 50 cents. Also for harmonizing Persian modes. I created the Persian chords; there is not something weird. There are same regular chords, but only in some chord s notes, there are quarter-tones and shows with this symbol (*). Example M(3*) a major chord with a quarter-tone in third. Alternatively, 7(7*) SUS 4(4*)(5*) a 7sus4 chord with quarter-tones in fourth, fifth, seventh. The quarter-tone is just like a musical effect just a little banding guitar strings between a semi-tone interval.

M3 + m3 = Major	M
M3 + m3 + M3 = major7th / Δ7	MΔ7
M3 + m3 + m3 = Dominant7th / M7	M7
M3 + m3 + m3 + M3 = Dominant9th / M9	M9
M3 + m3 + m3 + m3 = Minor9th / m9	m9
P5 + m3 + M3 + m3 = Dominant11th	M11
M3 + d5 + M3 + P5 = Dominant13th	M13
M3 + d5 + M3 + d5 = Minor13th	m13
m3 + M3 = Minor	m
m3 + M3 + m3 = Minor7th / m7	m7
m3 + M3 + M3 = Minor Major7th / mΔ7	mΔ7
m3 + m3 = Diminishd	o
m3 + m3 + m3 = Full diminished7th / o7	o7
m3 + m3 + M3 = Half diminished7th / ø7	ø7
m3 + m3 + P4 = Diminished major7th / oΔ7	oΔ7
M3 + M3 = Augmented	+
M3 + M3 + M2 = Augmented7th / +7	+7
M3 + M3 + m3 = Augmented Major7th +Δ7	+Δ7
M3 + M2 = Major b5 m3 + P5 = Minorb5	

M3 + m3 + M2=Dominant6th /	M6
M2 + P4 = SUS2	
P4 + M2 = SUS4	

m3 + M3 + M2 = Minor6 / m6	m6

M3 + M2 = Major b5
M3 + M2 + P4 = Major Δ7 b5
M3 + M2 + M3 = Major 7 b5
M3 + M2 + m3 = Major 6 b5
m3 + P4 = Minor #5
m3 + P4 + m3 = Minor Δ7 #5
m3 + P4 + M2 = Minor 7 #5
m3 + P4 + m2 = Minor 6 #5

M2 + P4 = sus2	P4 + M2 = sus4
M2 + P4 + M3 = Δ7sus2	P4 + M2 + M3 = Δ7sus4
M2 + P4 + m3 = 7sus2	P4 + M2 + m2 = 7sus4
M2 + P4 + M2 = 6sus2	P4 + M2 + M2 = 6sus4
M2 + M3 = sus2 b5	P4 + m2 = sus4 b5
M2 + M3 + P4 = Δ7sus2 b5	P4 + m2 + P4 = Δ7sus4 b5
M2 + M3 + M3 = 7sus2 b5	P4 + m2 + M3 = 7sus4 b5
M2 + M3 + m3 = 6sus2 b5	P4 + m2 + M2 = 6sus4 b5
M2 + A4 = sus2 #5	P4 + m3 = sus4 #5
M2 + A4 + M3 = Δ7sus2 #5	P4 + m3 + m3 = Δ7sus4 #5
M2 + A4 + m3 = 7sus2 #5	P4 + m3 + M2 = 7sus4 #5
M2 + A4 + M2 = 6sus2 #5	P4 + m3 + m2 = 6sus4 #5

CHAPTER II
GUITAR
AS THE BRAIN
OF MUSIC

The brain of music

By seeing shred guitarists, you might think that they have started a technical show. However, the shred guitar is not a show; it shows the musician's skill and understanding of the bases and elements of the music. These are the foundations of a composer, these skills improve the brain and Open the mind for composing. Learn more about the music base helps you become a better composer Solo artist or better musician. The advantage of guitar in addition to technology is that the guitar is the best positional instrument. With more than 3.5 octaves and also easy transposition to another key signature, just by moving positions on the Fretboard. This way, after eliminating this chapter, you will be able to learn all the modes of the world in chapters III and IV.

This chapter includes all the basic positions for guitar. These positions are daily practices for each guitarist and guitar students. Also, starts with Memorize Notes on the Guitar Fretboard, Intervals, chords and arpeggios, basic scales and modes, and figured bass chords. So finally, the structure of the guitar positions will be stored in your mind. All positions are sorted and have a longitudinal and transverse relationship. Every line in the tables teaches a position, and each line has a relationship with the upper and lower lines, By learning these positions and knowing their differences and their relationship. You will be able to improve the music. Moreover, compassion on the guitar with all elements of a virtuoso solo artist, or shred guitarist make music with your technics and make new likes in your music piece.

Full guitar courses just on 12 pages for daily practices. First, make a practicing plan. Specify the training time in each section. Each day chose one tonic note or root position for your practices, and that day plays everything in this tone. First by practicing memorizing notes on the guitar fretboard, second play intervals third bare chords, fourth sweep arpeggios from the cords, fifth scales, sixth modes, seventh figured bass chords. After a few months, you will have significant progress. It is essential to lessen to the sound when you practice. Also, your practicing plan for this chapter can train your ears too. If you are singing with this practices and listen carefully to the sounds, you will get a better Result. Example day 1 is for note A on this day you should play all A notes first find all A notes on the Fretboard. After that practice interval with a root a tone. Take a lock to the pentatonic pattern; it is so essential everything has a revelation with it. Then practice chords for each chord there are five boxes, then five bares. After undressing chord shapes, you can use sweep arpeggio to memories them. So improve well. Each scale is divided into several boxes horizontally. So finally, vertically each scale is in a relationship with another scale. In the Continuing Learn Church modes in the same order. Moreover, at the end with the figurine bases expand your technical knowledge.

How to Memorize Notes on the Guitar Fretboard, it is better to learn the notes on the guitar fretboard with Practice unison and octave Intervals on a note. The music alphabet includes seven letters. and each week consists of 7 days. Learning the Notes on the guitar Fretboard is so easy. It Just needs 7 minutes each day. There are seven days a week and seven letters on music. Each day of the week is for one letter of the music alphabet. Practice you can play the A note as a tonic for all position, as arpeggios, two-handed tapping, chords, bare cords and more. Day 2 is for C, day 3 is for E, day 4 is for G, day 5 is for B, day 6 is for D, and day 7 is for F. After 2 weeks you can go on {sharp & flat} notes A#Bb - C#Db - F#Gb - G#Ab - D#Eb 5 tones for 5 days and for day 6 and 7 play all these 5 tones for each practice after 2 weeks change the tones.

Sequence numbers

After learning the scale and mode patterns. You need to use sequence numbers for practice. Moreover, improve your technical skills in scale and mode patterns. You can make scale sequences of any scale or mode, just by ordering the scale digress. Moreover, variations notes in sequences numbers. For making scale sequences of any scale or modes use sequence numbers in the next page.

▲ Sequence numbers with triple divisions

A (1-2-1 & 2-3-2 & ...) **B** (2-1-2 & 3-2-3 & ...)
C (1-2-3 & 2-3-4 & ...) **D** (3-2-1 & 4-3-2 & ...)
E (1-2-3 & 4-2-3 & ...) **F** (3-2-1 & 3-2-4 & ...)

■ Sequence numbers with quadruple divisions

A (1-2-3-4 & 2-3-4-5 & ...) **B** (4-3-2-1 & 5-4-3-2 & ...)
C (1-3-2-1 & 2-4-3-2 & ...) **D** (1-2-3-1 & 2-3-4-2 & ...)
E (1-3-2-4 & 3-5-4-6 & ...) **F** (4-2-3-1 & 6-4-5-3 & ...)
G (1-3-2-3 & 2-4-3-5 & ...) **H** (3-2-3-1 & 5-3-4-2 & ...)
I (2-1-2-3 & 4-3-4-5 & ...) **J** (3-2-1-2 & 5-4-3-4 & ...)
K (1-3-4-2 & 3-5-6-4 & ...) **L** (2-4-3-1 & 4-6-5-3 & ...)

⬢ Sequence numbers with Sextuplet divisions

A (1-2-3-4-5-6 & 2-3-4-5-6-7 & ...)
B (6-5-4-3-2-1 & 7-6-5-4-3-2 & ...)
C (1-2-3-4-2-3 & 4-5-3-4-5-6 & ...)
D (3-2-4-3-2-1 & 6-5-4-3-5-4 & ...)
E (3-1-3-2-4-2 & 3-5-3-4-6-4 & ...)
F (1-3-1 4-2-4 & 5-3-5-6-4-6 & ...)
G (1-4-3-2-4-5 & 2-5-4-3-5-6 & ...)
H (5-4-2-3-4-1 & 6-5-3-4-5-2 & ...)
I (1-3-2-4-6-5 & 2-4-3-5-7-6 & ...)
J (5-6-4-2-3-1 & 6-7-5-3-4-2 & ...)
K (1-3-2-4-3-5 & 6-5-4-5-4-3 & ...)
L (5-3-4-2-3-1 & 3-4-5-4-5-6 & ...)

The earth culture music rainbow

0	1&13	2&14	3&15	4&16	5&17	6&18	7&19	8&20	9&21	10&22	11&23	12&24
E	F	F#Gb	G	G#Ab	A	A#Bb	B	C	C#Db	D	D#Eb	E
B	C	C#Db	D	D#Eb	E	F	F#Gb	G	G#Ab	A	A#Bb	B
G	G#Ab	A	A#Bb	B	C	C#Db	D	D#Eb	E	F	F#Gb	G
D	D#Eb	E	F	F#Gb	G	G#Ab	A	A#Bb	B	C	C#Db	D
A	A#Bb	B	C	C#Db	D	D#Eb	E	F	F#Gb	G	G#Ab	A
E	F	F#Gb	G	G#Ab	A	A#Bb	B	C	C#Db	D	D#Eb	E
B	C	C#Db	D	D#Eb	E	F	F#Gb	G	G#Ab	A	A#Bb	B

0	1&13	2&14	3&15	4&16	5&17	6&18	7&19	8&20	9&21	10&22	11&23	12&24
E	F	F#Gb	G	G#Ab	A	A#Bb	B	C	C#Db	D	D#Eb	E
B	C	C#Db	D	D#Eb	E	F	F#Gb	G	G#Ab	A	A#Bb	B
G	G#Ab	A	A#Bb	B	C	C#Db	D	D#Eb	E	F	F#Gb	G
D	D#Eb	E	F	F#Gb	G	G#Ab	A	A#Bb	B	C	C#Db	D
A	A#Bb	B	C	C#Db	D	D#Eb	E	F	F#Gb	G	G#Ab	A
E	F	F#Gb	G	G#Ab	A	A#Bb	B	C	C#Db	D	D#Eb	E
B	C	C#Db	D	D#Eb	E	F	F#Gb	G	G#Ab	A	A#Bb	B

0	1&13	2&14	3&15	4&16	5&17	6&18	7&19	8&20	9&21	10&22	11&23	12&24
E	F	F#Gb	G	G#Ab	A	A#Bb	B	C	C#Db	D	D#Eb	E
B	C	C#Db	D	D#Eb	E	F	F#Gb	G	G#Ab	A	A#Bb	B
G	G#Ab	A	A#Bb	B	C	C#Db	D	D#Eb	E	F	F#Gb	G
D	D#Eb	E	F	F#Gb	G	G#Ab	A	A#Bb	B	C	C#Db	D
A	A#Bb	B	C	C#Db	D	D#Eb	E	F	F#Gb	G	G#Ab	A
E	F	F#Gb	G	G#Ab	A	A#Bb	B	C	C#Db	D	D#Eb	E
B	C	C#Db	D	D#Eb	E	F	F#Gb	G	G#Ab	A	A#Bb	B

0	1&13	2&14	3&15	4&16	5&17	6&18	7&19	8&20	9&21	10&22	11&23	12&24
E	F	F#Gb	G	G#Ab	A	A#Bb	B	C	C#Db	D	D#Eb	E
B	C	C#Db	D	D#Eb	E	F	F#Gb	G	G#Ab	A	A#Bb	B
G	G#Ab	A	A#Bb	B	C	C#Db	D	D#Eb	E	F	F#Gb	G
D	D#Eb	E	F	F#Gb	G	G#Ab	A	A#Bb	B	C	C#Db	D
A	A#Bb	B	C	C#Db	D	D#Eb	E	F	F#Gb	G	G#Ab	A
E	F	F#Gb	G	G#Ab	A	A#Bb	B	C	C#Db	D	D#Eb	E
B	C	C#Db	D	D#Eb	E	F	F#Gb	G	G#Ab	A	A#Bb	B

0	1&13	2&14	3&15	4&16	5&17	6&18	7&19	8&20	9&21	10&22	11&23	12&24
E	F	F#Gb	G	G#Ab	A	A#Bb	B	C	C#Db	D	D#Eb	E
B	C	C#Db	D	D#Eb	E	F	F#Gb	G	G#Ab	A	A#Bb	B
G	G#Ab	A	A#Bb	B	C	C#Db	D	D#Eb	E	F	F#Gb	G
D	D#Eb	E	F	F#Gb	G	G#Ab	A	A#Bb	B	C	C#Db	D
A	A#Bb	B	C	C#Db	D	D#Eb	E	F	F#Gb	G	G#Ab	A
E	F	F#Gb	G	G#Ab	A	A#Bb	B	C	C#Db	D	D#Eb	E
B	C	C#Db	D	D#Eb	E	F	F#Gb	G	G#Ab	A	A#Bb	B

0	1&13	2&14	3&15	4&16	5&17	6&18	7&19	8&20	9&21	10&22	11&23	12&24
E	F	F#Gb	G	G#Ab	A	A#Bb	B	C	C#Db	D	D#Eb	
A	A#Bb	B	C	C#Db	D	D#Eb	E	E	F	F#Gb	G	G#Ab
E	F	F#Gb	G	G#Ab	A	A#Bb	B	B	C	C#Db	D	D#Eb
C	C#Db	D	D#Eb	E	F	F#Gb	G	G	G#Ab	A	A#Bb	B
G	G#Ab	A	A#Bb	B	C	C#Db	D	D	D#Eb	E	F	F#Gb
D	D#Eb	E	F	F#Gb	G	G#Ab	A	A	A#Bb	B	C	C#Db
A	A#Bb	B	C	C#Db	D	D#Eb	E	E	F	F#Gb	G	G#Ab
								B	C	C#Db	D	D#Eb

0	1&13	2&14	3&15	4&16	5&17	6&18	7&19	8&20	9&21	10&22	11&23	12&24
E	F	F#Gb	G	G#Ab	A	A#Bb	B	C	C#Db	D	D#Eb	E
B	C	C#Db	D	D#Eb	E	F	F#Gb	G	G#Ab	A	A#Bb	B
G	G#Ab	A	A#Bb	B	C	C#Db	D	D#Eb	E	F	F#Gb	G
D	D#Eb	E	F	F#Gb	G	G#Ab	A	A#Bb	B	C	C#Db	D
A	A#Bb	B	C	C#Db	D	D#Eb	E	F	F#Gb	G	G#Ab	A
E	F	F#Gb	G	G#Ab	A	A#Bb	B	C	C#Db	D	D#Eb	E
B	C	C#Db	D	D#Eb	E	F	F#Gb	G	G#Ab	A	A#Bb	B

0	1&13	2&14	3&15	4&16	5&17	6&18	7&19	8&20	9&21	10&22	11&23	12&24
E	F	F#Gb	G	G#Ab	A	A#Bb	B	C	C#Db	D	D#Eb	E
B	C	C#Db	D	D#Eb	E	F	F#Gb	G	G#Ab	A	A#Bb	B
G	G#Ab	A	A#Bb	B	C	C#Db	D	D#Eb	E	F	F#Gb	G
D	D#Eb	E	F	F#Gb	G	G#Ab	A	A#Bb	B	C	C#Db	D
A	A#Bb	B	C	C#Db	D	D#Eb	E	F	F#Gb	G	G#Ab	A
E	F	F#Gb	G	G#Ab	A	A#Bb	B	C	C#Db	D	D#Eb	E
B	C	C#Db	D	D#Eb	E	F	F#Gb	G	G#Ab	A	A#Bb	B

0	1&13	2&14	3&15	4&16	5&17	6&18	7&19	8&20	9&21	10&22	11&23	12&24
E	F	F#Gb	G	G#Ab	A	A#Bb	B	C	C#Db	D	D#Eb	E
B	C	C#Db	D	D#Eb	E	F	F#Gb	G	G#Ab	A	A#Bb	B
G	G#Ab	A	A#Bb	B	C	C#Db	D	D#Eb	E	F	F#Gb	G
D	D#Eb	E	F	F#Gb	G	G#Ab	A	A#Bb	B	C	C#Db	D
A	A#Bb	B	C	C#Db	D	D#Eb	E	F	F#Gb	G	G#Ab	A
E	F	F#Gb	G	G#Ab	A	A#Bb	B	C	C#Db	D	D#Eb	E
B	C	C#Db	D	D#Eb	E	F	F#Gb	G	G#Ab	A	A#Bb	B

0	1&13	2&14	3&15	4&16	5&17	6&18	7&19	8&20	9&21	10&22	11&23	12&24
E	F	F#Gb	G	G#Ab	A	A#Bb	B	C	C#Db	D	D#Eb	E
B	C	C#Db	D	D#Eb	E	F	F#Gb	G	G#Ab	A	A#Bb	B
G	G#Ab	A	A#Bb	B	C	C#Db	D	D#Eb	E	F	F#Gb	G
D	D#Eb	E	F	F#Gb	G	G#Ab	A	A#Bb	B	C	C#Db	D
A	A#Bb	B	C	C#Db	D	D#Eb	E	F	F#Gb	G	G#Ab	A
E	F	F#Gb	G	G#Ab	A	A#Bb	B	C	C#Db	D	D#Eb	E
B	C	C#Db	D	D#Eb	E	F	F#Gb	G	G#Ab	A	A#Bb	B

0	1&13	2&14	3&15	4&16	5&17	6&18	7&19	8&20	9&21	10&22	11&23	12&24
E	F	F#Gb	G	G#Ab	A	A#Bb	B	C	C#Db	D	D#Eb	E
B	C	C#Db	D	D#Eb	E	F	F#Gb	G	G#Ab	A	A#Bb	B
G	G#Ab	A	A#Bb	B	C	C#Db	D	D#Eb	E	F	F#Gb	G
D	D#Eb	E	F	F#Gb	G	G#Ab	A	A#Bb	B	C	C#Db	D
A	A#Bb	B	C	C#Db	D	D#Eb	E	F	F#Gb	G	G#Ab	A
E	F	F#Gb	G	G#Ab	A	A#Bb	B	C	C#Db	D	D#Eb	E
B	C	C#Db	D	D#Eb	E	F	F#Gb	G	G#Ab	A	A#Bb	B

0	1&13	2&14	3&15	4&16	5&17	6&18	7&19	8&20	9&21	10&22	11&23	12&24
E	F	F#Gb	G	G#Ab	A	A#Bb	B	C	C#Db	D	D#Eb	E
B	C	C#Db	D	D#Eb	E	F	F#Gb	G	G#Ab	A	A#Bb	B
G	G#Ab	A	A#Bb	B	C	C#Db	D	D#Eb	E	F	F#Gb	G
D	D#Eb	E	F	F#Gb	G	G#Ab	A	A#Bb	B	C	C#Db	D
A	A#Bb	B	C	C#Db	D	D#Eb	E	F	F#Gb	G	G#Ab	A
E	F	F#Gb	G	G#Ab	A	A#Bb	B	C	C#Db	D	D#Eb	E
B	C	C#Db	D	D#Eb	E	F	F#Gb	G	G#Ab	A	A#Bb	B

Full fretboard notes diagram and equivalent frets

0	1&13	2&14	3&15	4&16	5&17	6&18	7&19	8&20	9&21	10&22	11&23	12&24
E	F	F#Gb	G	G#Ab	A	A#Bb	B	C	C#Db	D	D#Eb	E
B	C	C#Db	D	D#Eb	E	F	F#Gb	G	G#Ab	A	A#Bb	B
G	G#Ab	A	A#Bb	B	C	C#Db	D	D#Eb	E	F	F#Gb	G
D	D#Eb	E	F	F#Gb	G	G#Ab	A	A#Bb	B	C	C#Db	D
A	A#Bb	B	C	C#Db	D	D#Eb	E	F	F#Gb	G	G#Ab	A
E	F	F#Gb	G	G#Ab	A	A#Bb	B	C	C#Db	D	D#Eb	E
B	C	C#Db	D	D#Eb	E	F	F#Gb	G	G#Ab	A	A#Bb	B

Frets notes

1 & 13: F, C, G#Ab, D#Eb, A#Bb, F, C

3 & 15: G, D, A#Bb, F, C, G, D

5 & 17: A, E, C, G, D, A, E

7 & 19: B, F#Gb, D, A, E, B, F#Gb

9 & 21: C#Db, G#Ab, E, B, F#Gb, C#Db, G#Ab

11 & 23: D#Eb, A#Bb, F#Gb, C#Db, G#Ab, D#Eb, A#Bb

2 & 14: F#Gb, C#Db, A, E, B, F#Gb, C#Db

4 & 16: G#Ab, D#Eb, B, F#Gb, C#Db, G#Ab, D#Eb

6 & 18: A#Bb, F, C#Db, G#Ab, D#Eb, A#Bb, F

8 & 20: C, G, D#Eb, A#Bb, F, C, G

10 & 22: D, A, F, C, G, D, A

0 / 12 & 24: E, B, G, D, A, E, B

Diagrams study guide

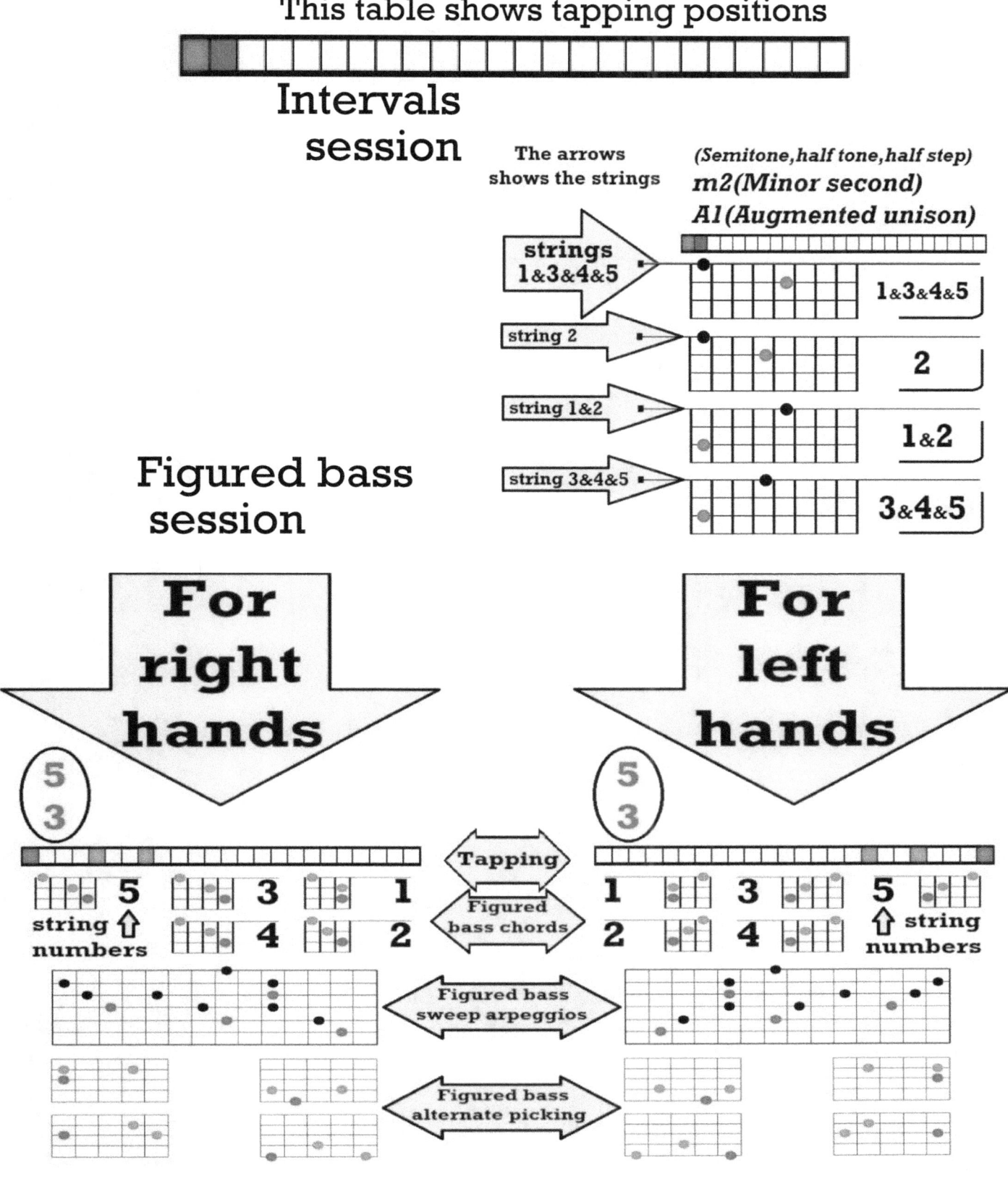

BASIC POSITIONS FOR RIGHT-HANDS

P1 (Perfect unison)
d2 (Diminished second)

(Semitone, half tone, half step)
m2 (Minor second)
A1 (Augmented unison)

1 & 3 & 4 & 5
2
1 & 2
3 & 4 & 5

(Tone, whole tone, whole step)
M2 (Major second)
d3 (Diminished third)

m3 (Minor third)
A2 (Augmented second)

M3 (Major third)
d4 (Diminished fourth)

P4 (Perfect fourth)
A3 (Augmented third)

(Tritone)
d5 (Diminished fifth)
A4 (Augmented fourth)

P5 (Perfect fifth)
d6 (Diminished sixth)

m6 (Minor sixth)
A5 (Augmented fifth)

M6 (Major sixth)
d7 (Diminished seventh)

m7 (Minor seventh)
A6 (Augmented sixth)

M7 (Major seventh)
d8 (Diminished octave)

P8 (Perfect octave)
A7 (Augmented seventh)

Chord Shapes on Boxes

● = **Root** Chord
● = **Third** Chord
● = **Fifth** Chord

● Major tone

Positions	BOX 1	BOX 2	BOX 3	BOX 4	BOX 5	BOX 6
Pentatonic Positions						
Major Bar Chord Shapes on box positions						
Minor Bar Chord Shapes on box positions						
Major root / Minor root						
Major Bar Chord Shapes on box positions						
Figured Bass Triad Inversions						
Major triad root-position 5/3						
Major triad first-inversion 6/3						
Major triad second-inversion 6/4						
Minor Bar Chord Shapes on box positions						
Figured Bass Triad Inversions						
Minor triad root-position 5/3						
Minor triad first-inversion 6/3						
Minor triad second-inversion 6/4						

basic scale patterns

basic scale patterns on boxes

	BOX 1	BOX 2	BOX 3	BOX 4	BOX 5	BOX 6
Pentatonic						
Hexatonic Blues						
Heptatonic						
Harmonic minor						
Harmonic Major						
Jazz Melodic Minor						
Diminished						
Diminished Arpegios						
Whole-tone						
Whole-tone Arpegios						

Basic Modes

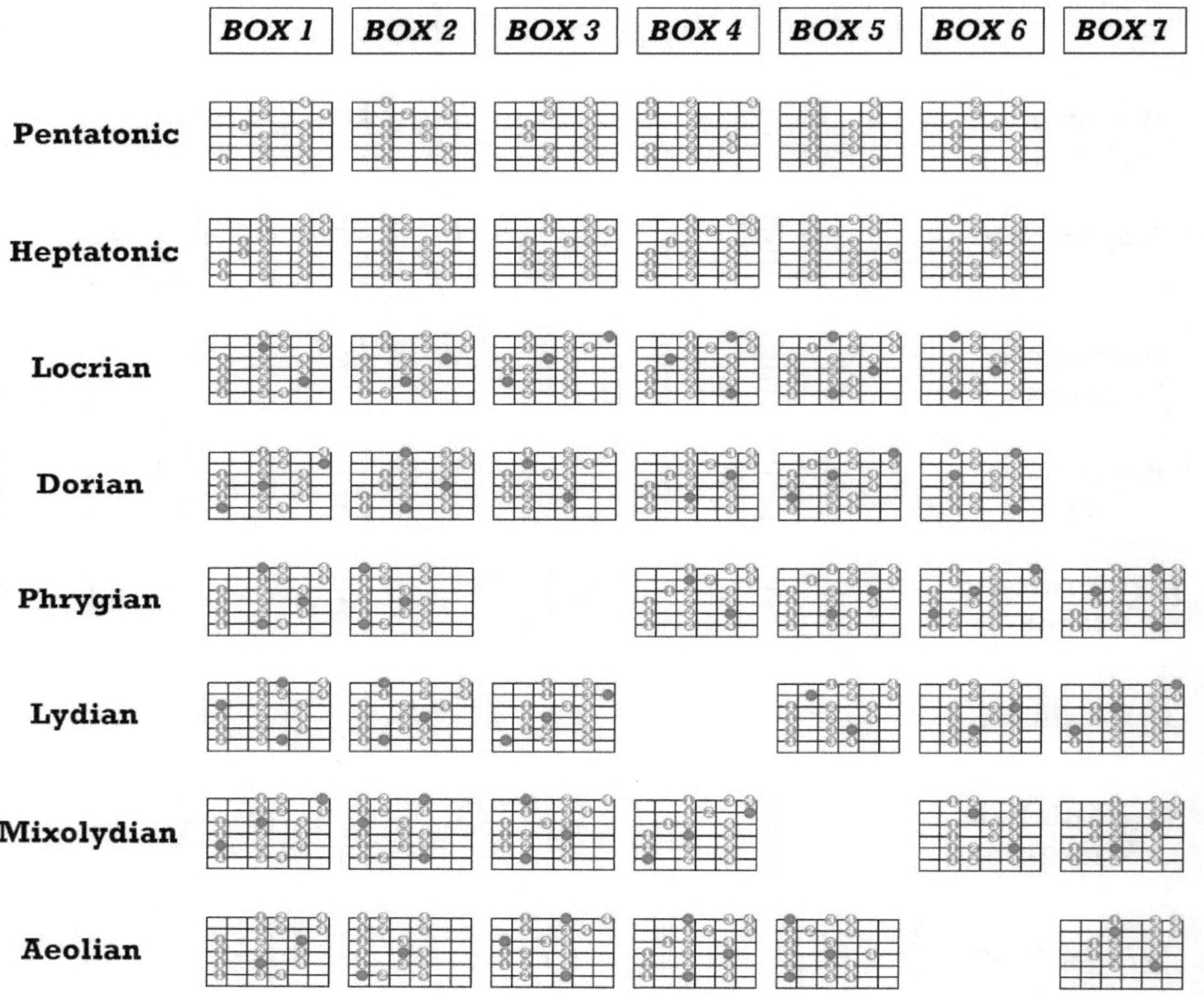

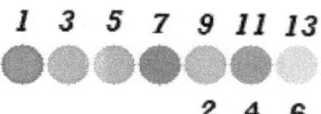

Octaves

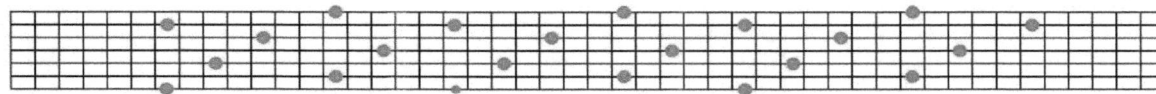

Major
M3 + m3 =

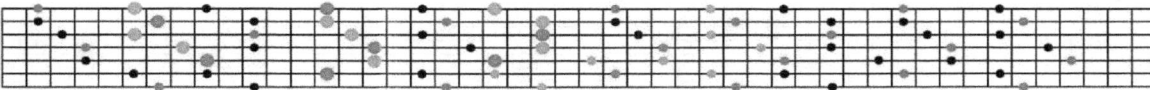

Major7th △ Maj7
M3 + m3 + M3 =

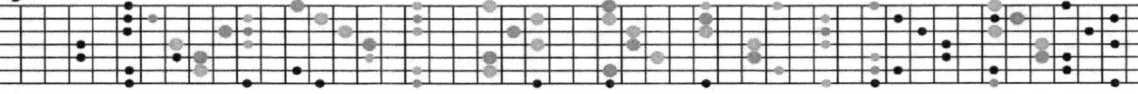

7 or Dominant7th
M3 + m3 + m3 =

9 or Dominant9th
M3 + m3 + m3 + M3 =

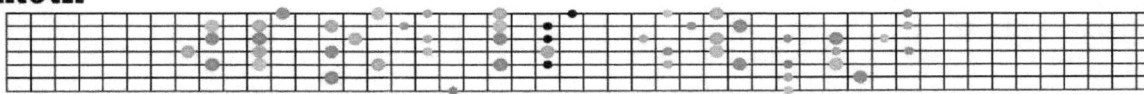

Minor9th
M3 + m3 + m3 + m3 =

11 Dominant11th
M3 + m3 + m3 + M3 + m3 =

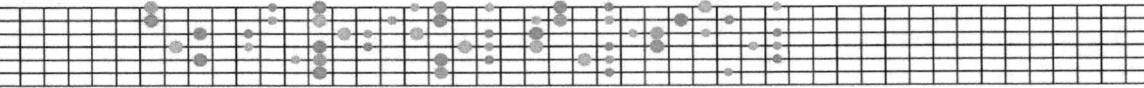

Dominant13th

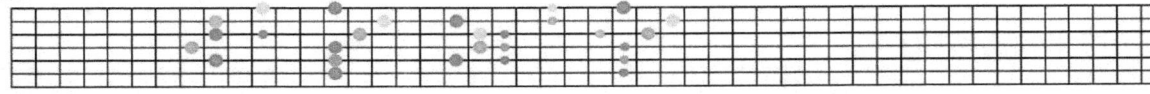

Minor13th

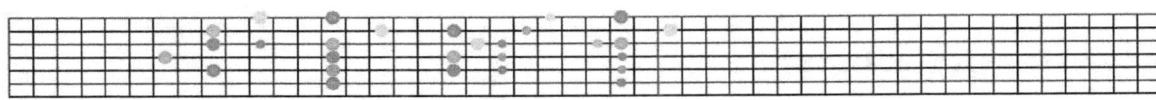

Minor
m3 + M3 =

7min Minor7th
m3 + M3 + m3 =

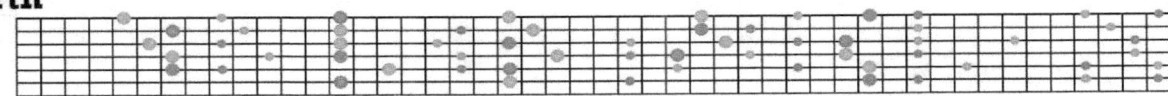

Minor 6
m3 + M3 + M2 =

arpeggios

Octaves

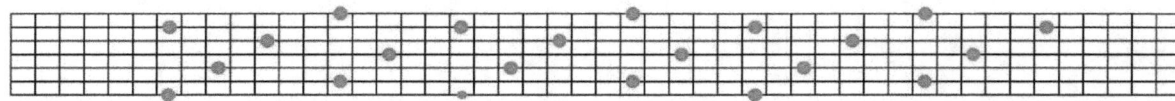

Diminished
m3 + m3 =

Half Diminished 7th
m3 + m3 + M3 =

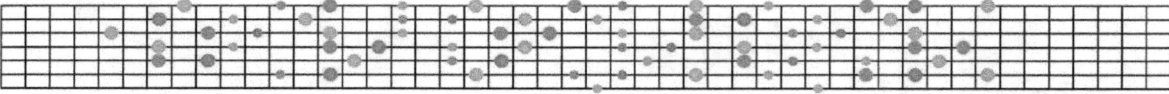

Full Diminished 7th
m3 + m3 + m3 =

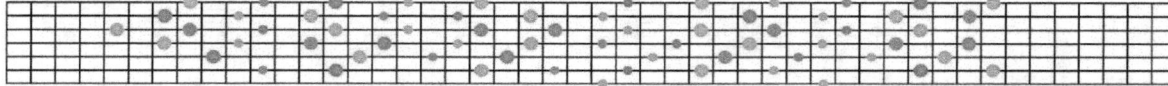

Augmented
M3 + M3 =

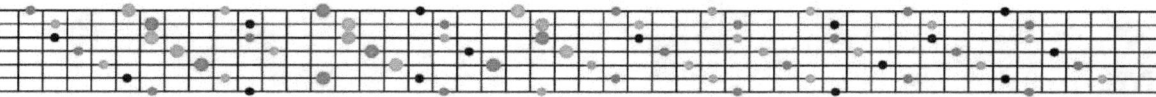

Dominant 7th
M3 + M3 + m3 =

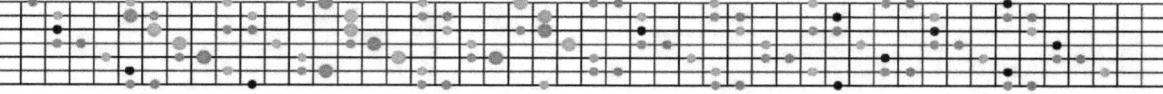

Augmented 7th
M3 + M3 + M2 =

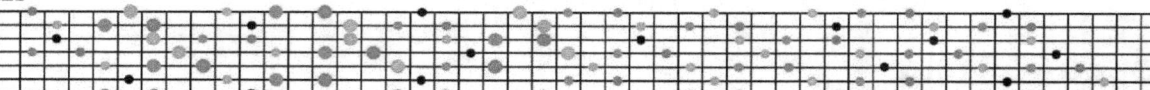

Major 7th △ Maj7
M3 + m3 + M3 =

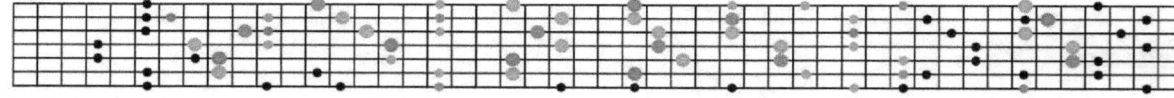

Mjor 7th with Minor 5th
m3 + M3 + M3 =

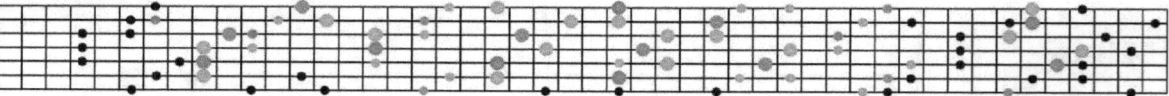

7 or Dominant 7th
M3 + m3 + m3 =

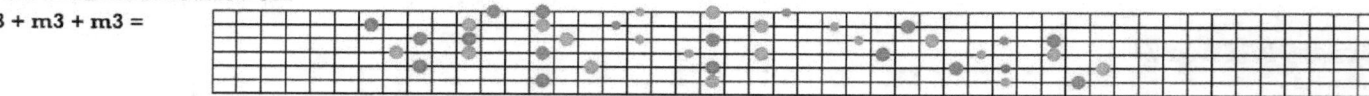

6 Dominant 6th
M3 + m3 + M2 =

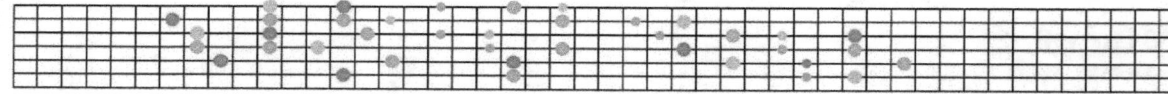

Octaves

9 or Dominant9th
M3 + m3 + m3 + M3 =

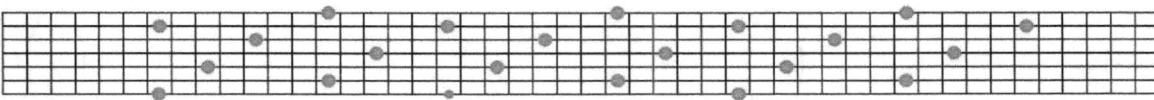

SUS 2
M2 + P4 =

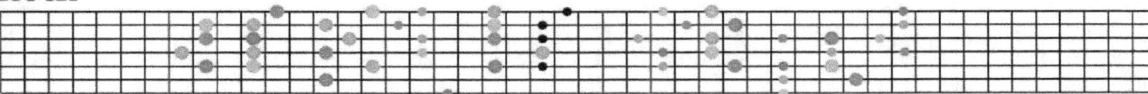

11 Dominant11th
M3 + m3 + m3 + M3
+ m3 =

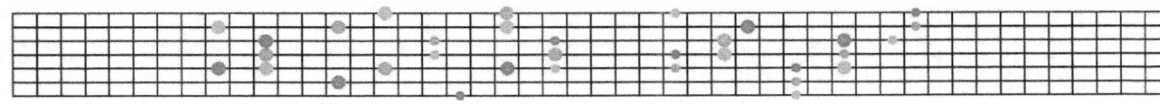

SUS 4
p4 + 2m =

Major

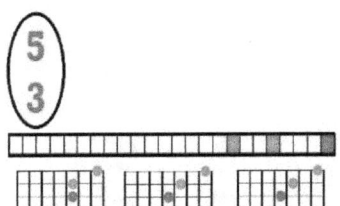   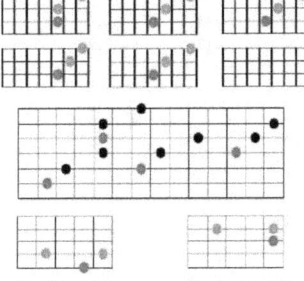 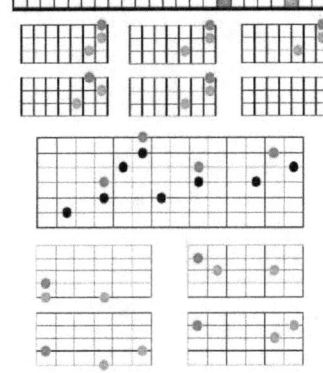 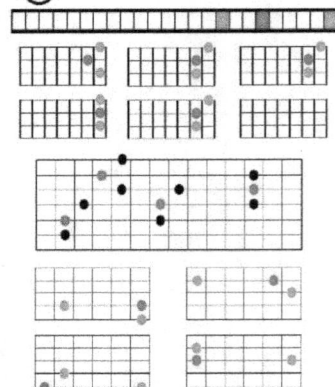

Major7th △ Maj7

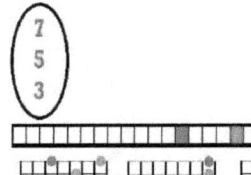 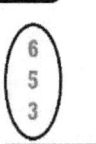 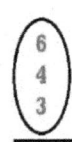 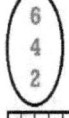 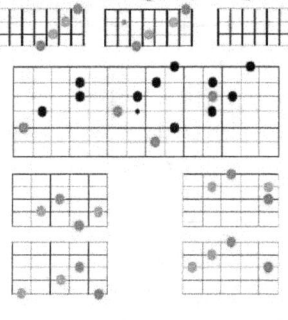 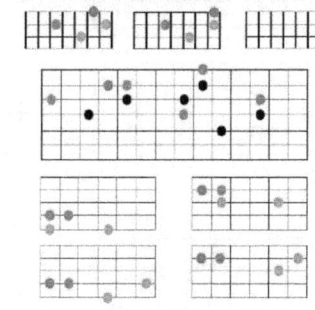 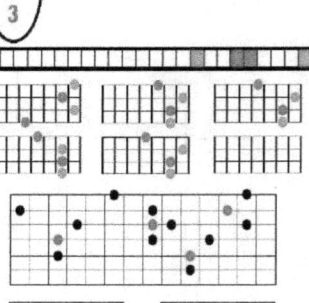 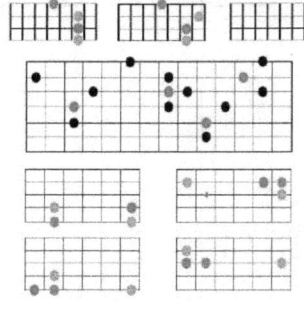 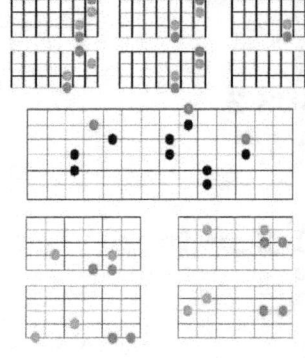

Dominant7th

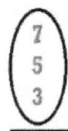 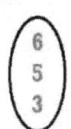 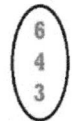 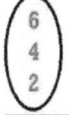 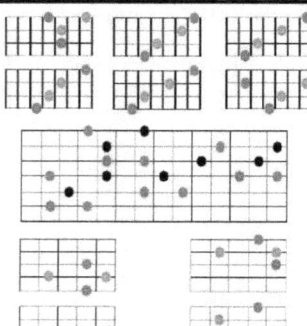 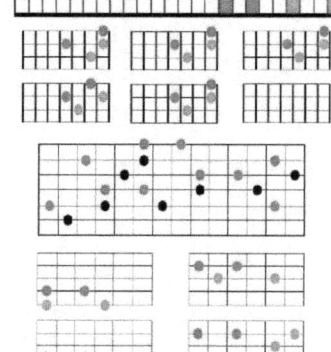 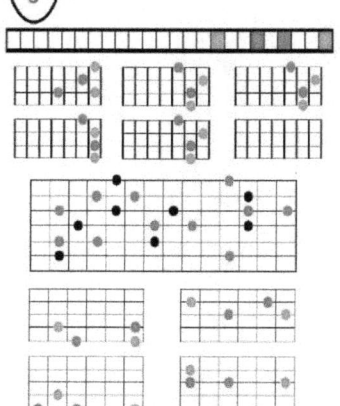

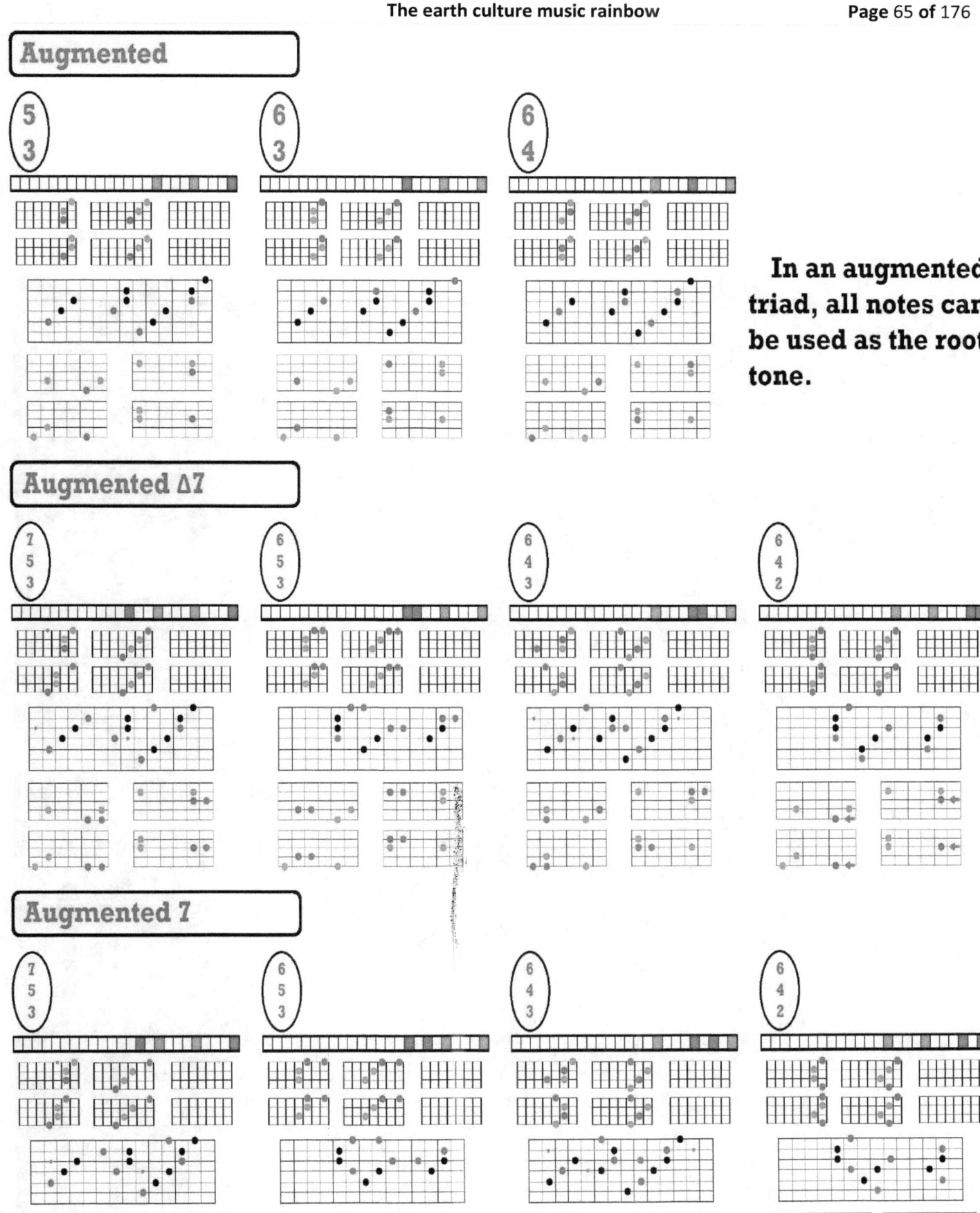

Minor

Minor 7

Minor Δ7

Diminished

 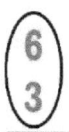  

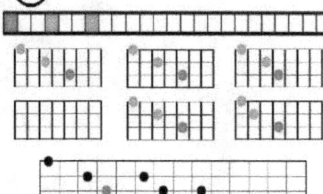
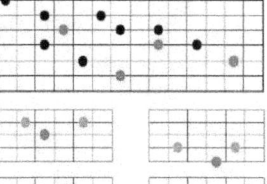
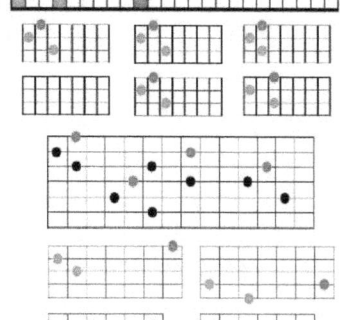
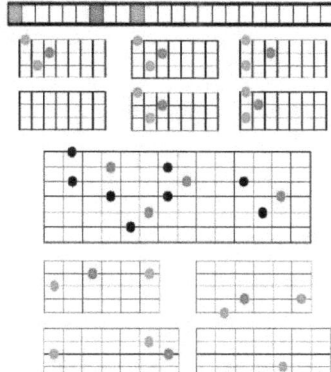

Half Diminished 7th

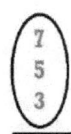 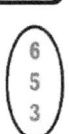 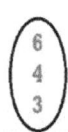 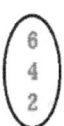

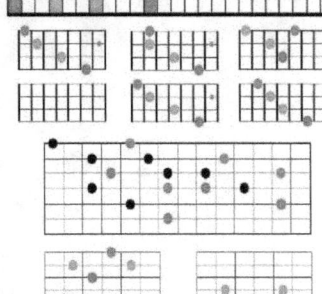
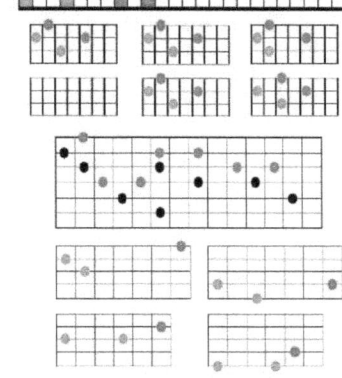
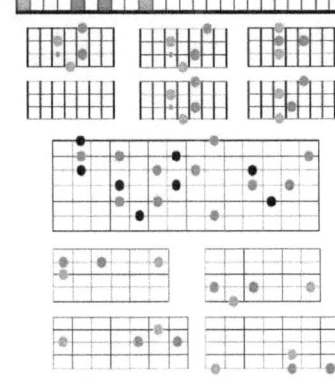
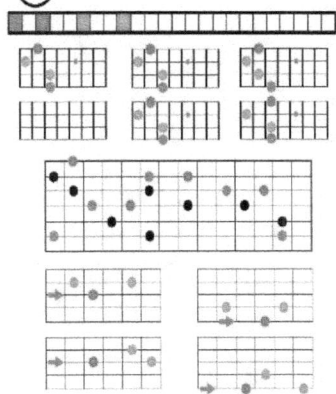

Full Diminished 7th

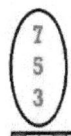 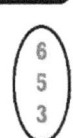 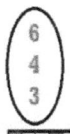 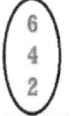

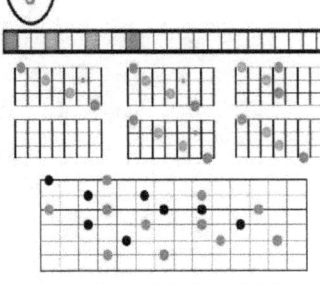
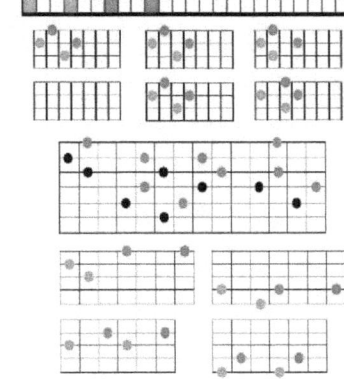
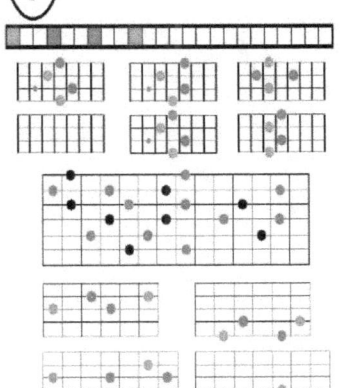
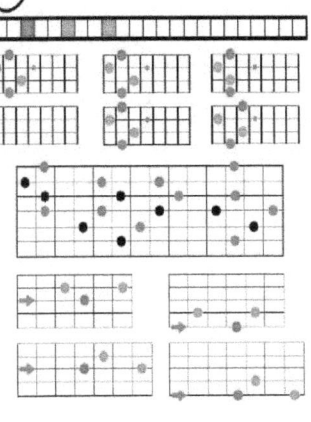

BASIC POSITIONS FOR LEFT-HANDS

The earth culture music rainbow

P1 (Perfect unison)
d2 (Diminished second)

---

m2 (Minor second)
A1 (Augmented unison)
(Semitone, half tone, half step)

1 & 3 & 4 & 5
2
1 & 2
3 & 4 & 5

M2 (Major second)
d3 (Diminished third)
(Tone, whole tone, whole step)

m3 (Minor third)
A2 (Augmented second)

M3 (Major third)
d4 (Diminished fourth)

P4 (Perfect fourth)
A3 (Augmented third)

d5 (Diminished fifth)
A4 (Augmented fourth)
(Tritone)

P5 (Perfect fifth)
d6 (Diminished sixth)

m6 (Minor sixth)
A5 (Augmented fifth)

M6 (Major sixth)
d7 (Diminished seventh)

m7 (Minor seventh)
A6 (Augmented sixth)

M7 (Major seventh)
d8 (Diminished octave)

P8 (Perfect octave)
A7 (Augmented seventh)

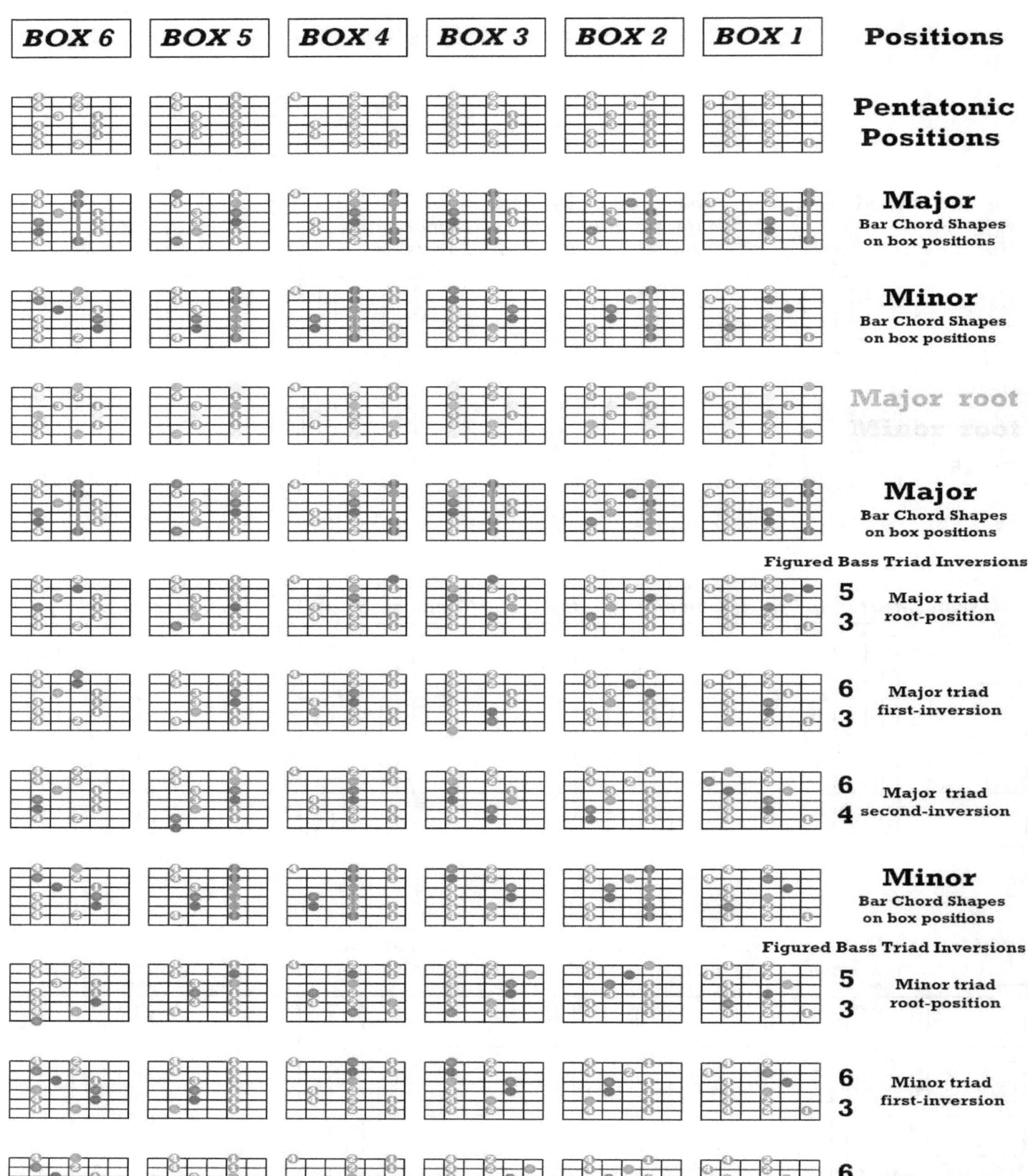

basic scale patterns

basic scale patterns on boxes

BOX 6	BOX 5	BOX 4	BOX 3	BOX 2	BOX 1	
						Pentatonic
						Hexatonic Blues
						Heptatonic
						Harmonic minor
						Harmonic Major
						Jazz Melodic Minor
						Diminished
						Diminished Arpegios
						Whole-tone
						Whole-tone Arpegios

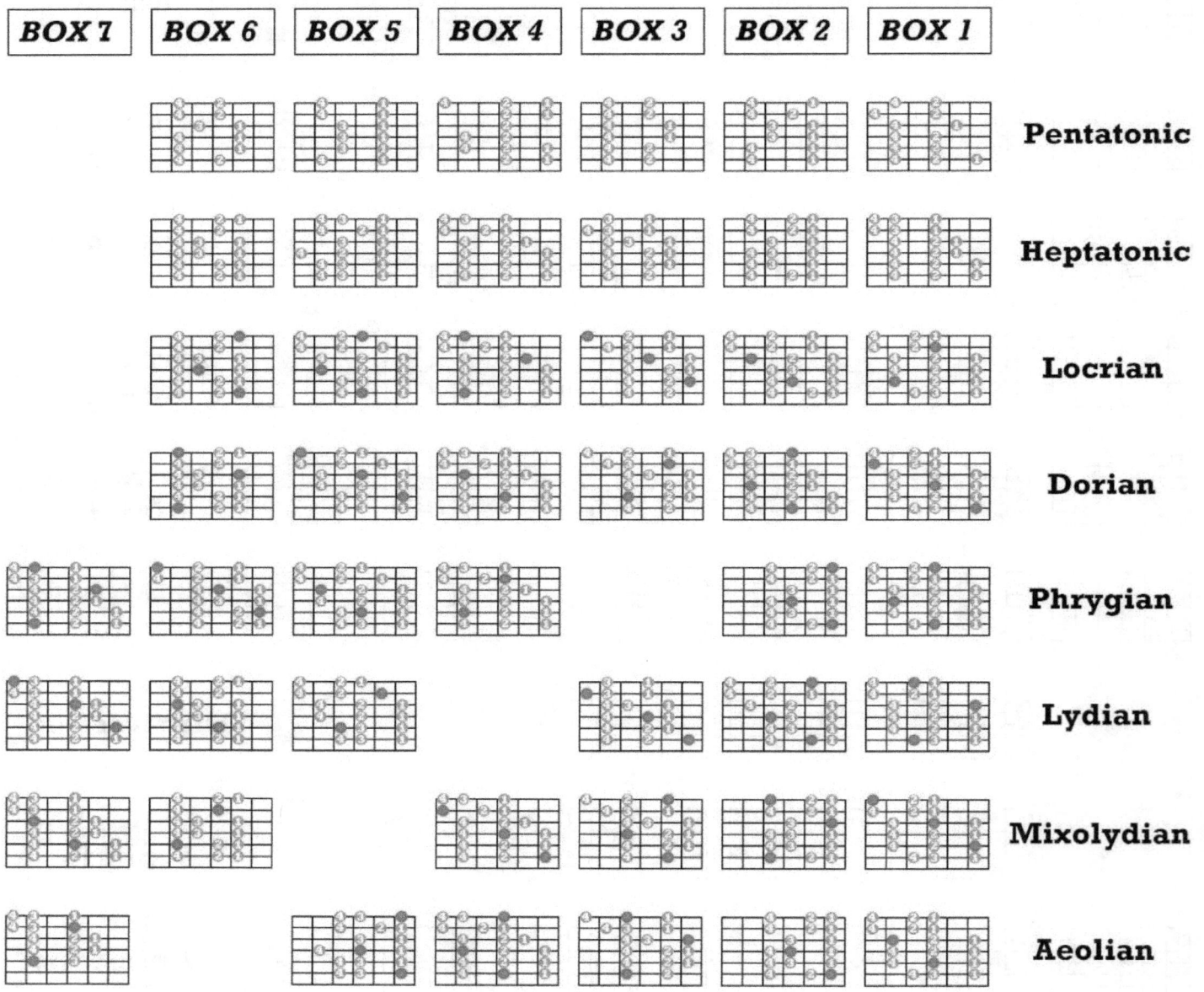

arpeggios

1 3 5 7 9 11 13

2 4 6

Octaves

Major
M3 + m3 =

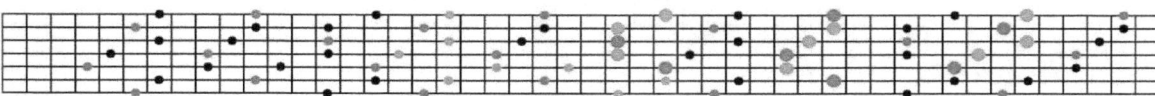

Major7th △ Maj7
M3 + m3 + M3 =

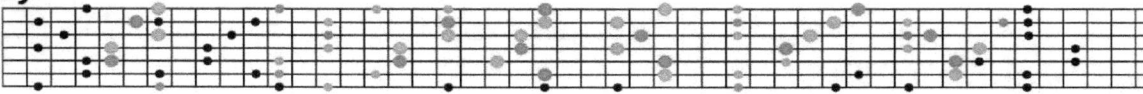

7 or Dominant7th
M3 + m3 + m3 =

9 or Dominant9th
M3 + m3 + m3 + M3 =

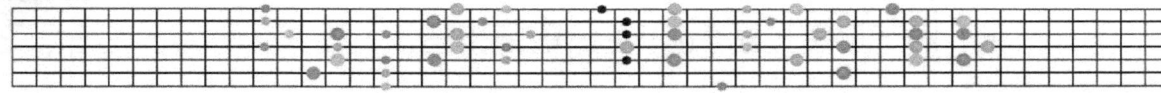

Minor9th
M3 + m3 + m3 + m3 =

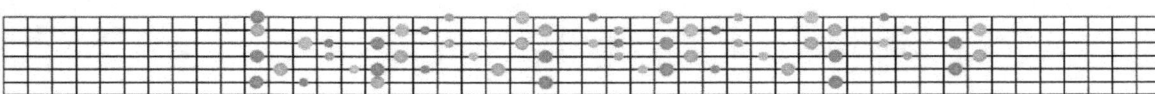

11 Dominant11th
M3 + m3 + m3 + M3 + m3 =

Dominant13th

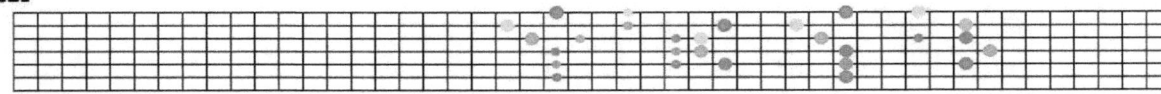

Minor13th

Minor
m3 + M3 =

7min Minor7th
m3 + M3 + m3 =

Minor 6
m3 + M3 + M2 =

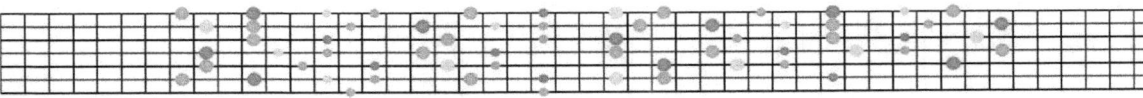

arpeggios

1 3 5 7 9 11 13

2 4 6

Octaves

Diminished
m3 + m3 =

Half Diminished7th
m3 + m3 + M3 =

Full Diminished7th
m3 + m3 + m3 =

Augmented
M3 + M3 =

Dominant 7th
M3 + M3 + m3 =

Augmented7th
M3 + M3 + M2 =

Major7th △ Maj7
M3 + m3 + M3 =

Mjor 7th with Minor 5th
m3 + M3 + M3 =

7 or Dominant7th
M3 + m3 + m3 =

6 Dominant6th
M3 + m3 + M2 =

1 3 5 7 9 11 13

2 4 6

Octaves

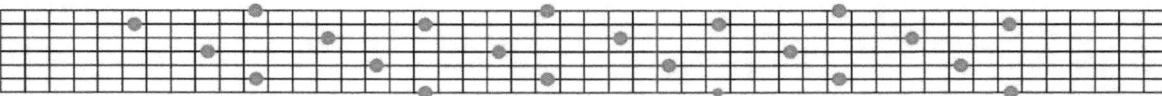

9 or Dominant9th
M3 + m3 + m3 + M3 =

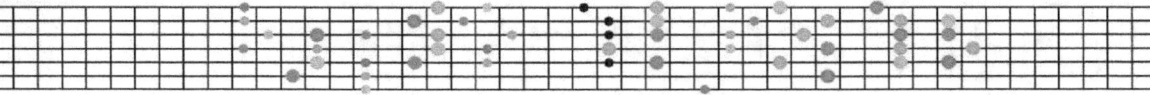

SUS 2
M2 + P4 =

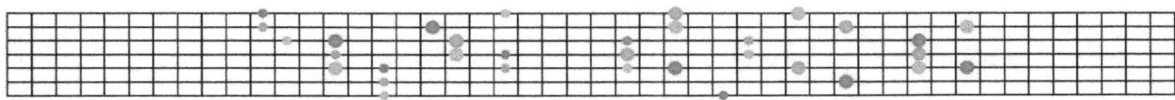

11 Dominant11th
M3 + m3 + m3 + M3
+ m3 =

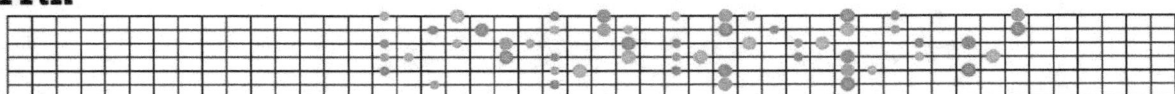

SUS 4
p4 + 2m =

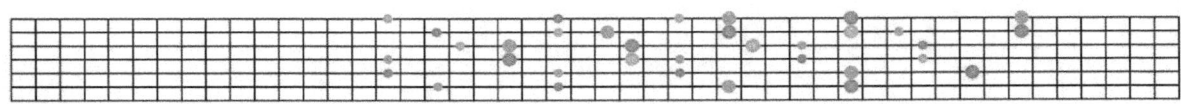

Major

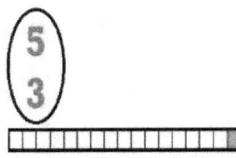  
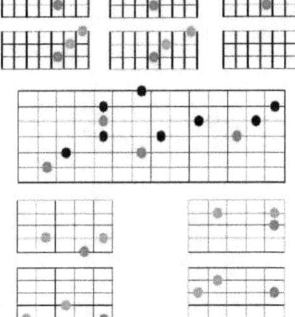 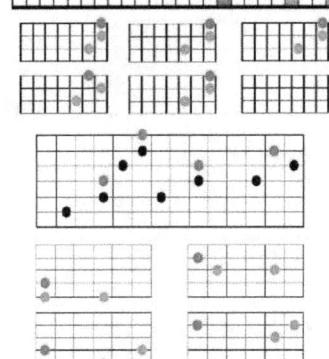 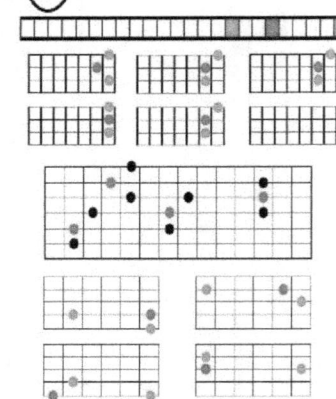

Major7th Δ Maj7

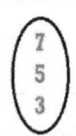 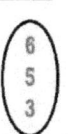 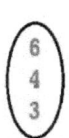 
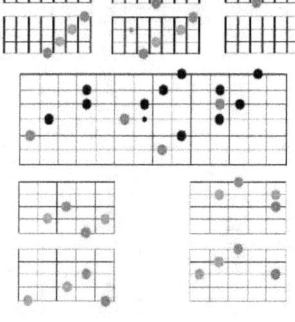 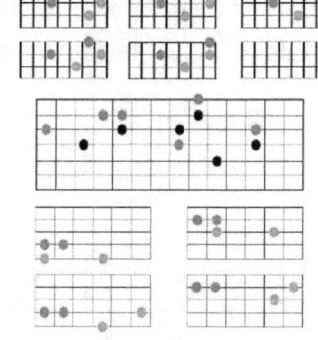 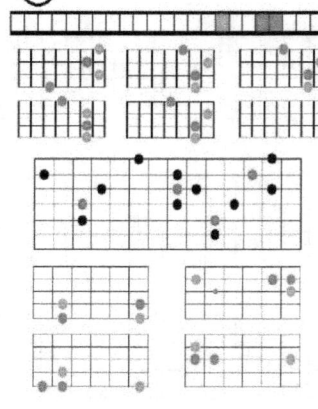 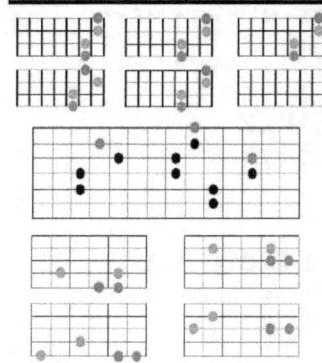

Dominant7th

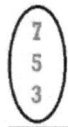 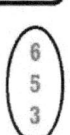 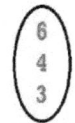 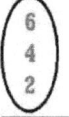
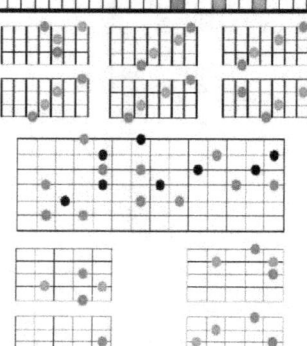 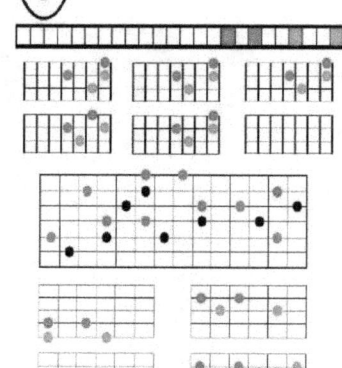 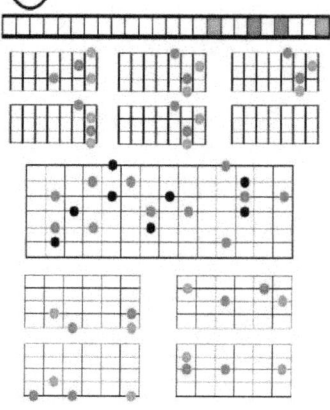

Augmented

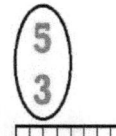  

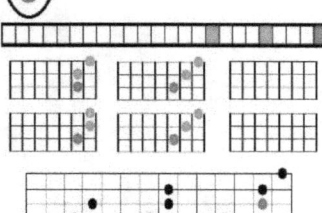
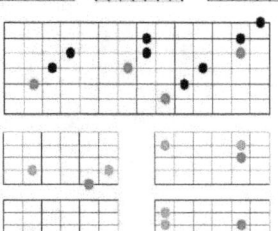
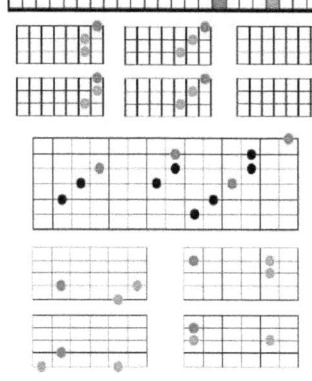
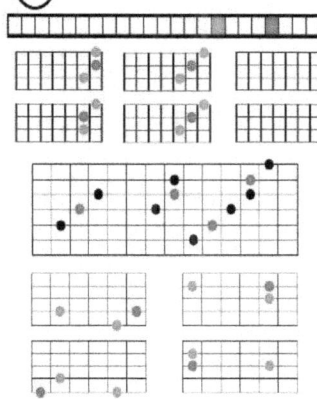

In an augmented triad, all notes can be used as the root tone.

Augmented Δ7

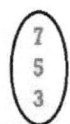 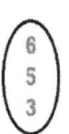 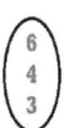 

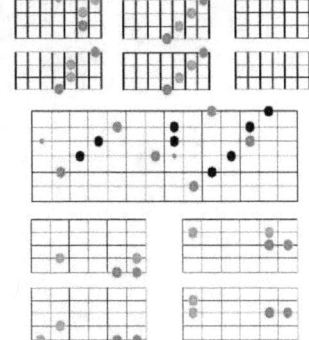
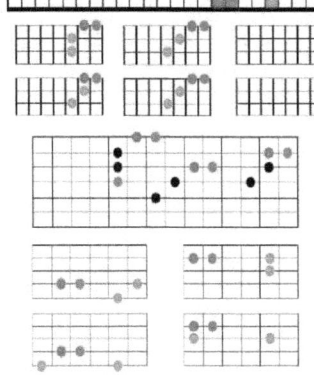
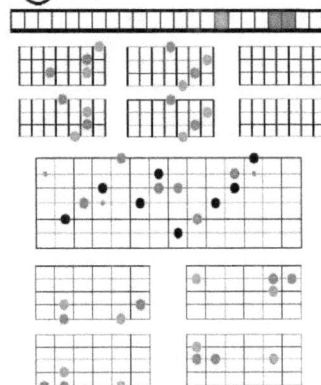
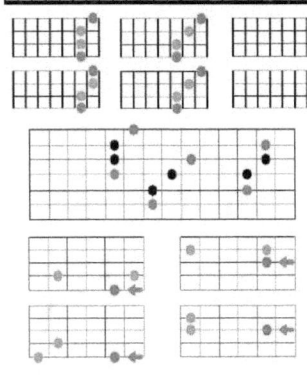

Augmented 7

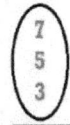 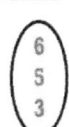 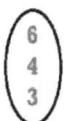 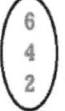

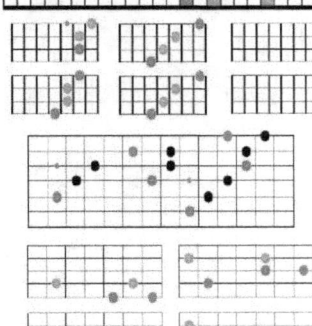
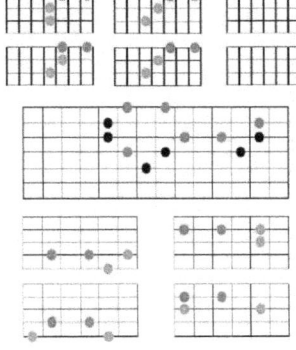
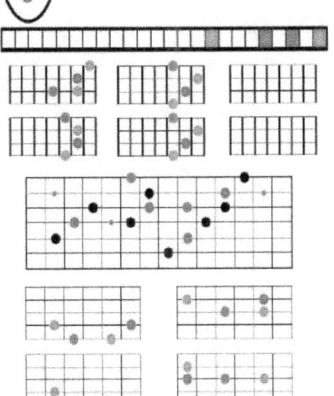
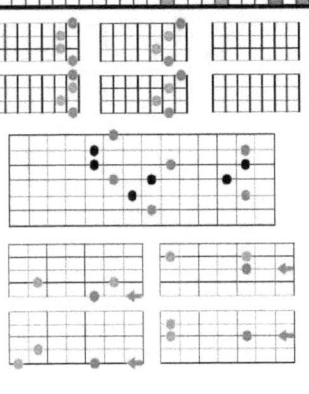

Minor

Minor 7

Minor Δ7

Diminished

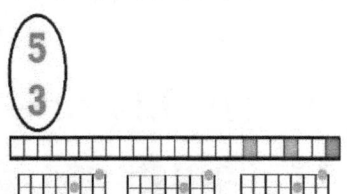
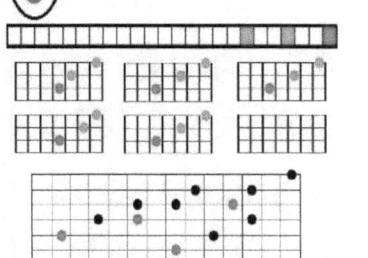
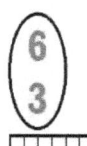
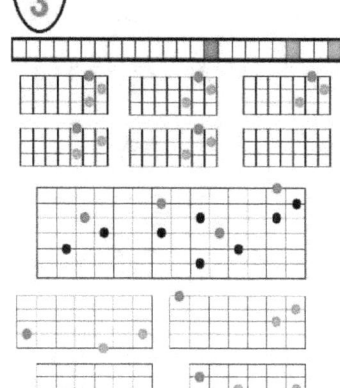

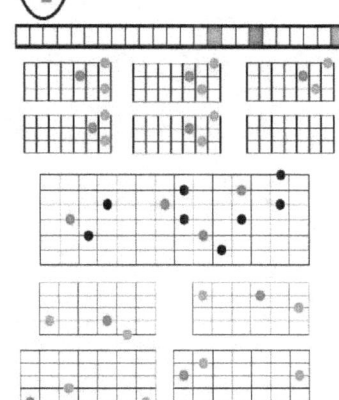

Half Diminished 7th

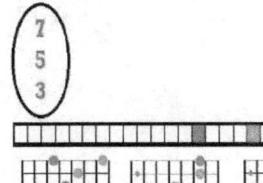
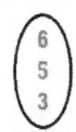
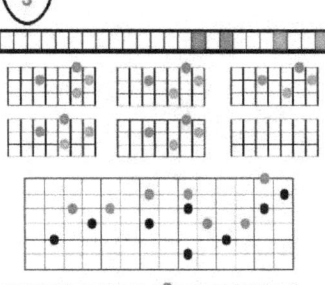
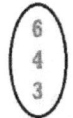
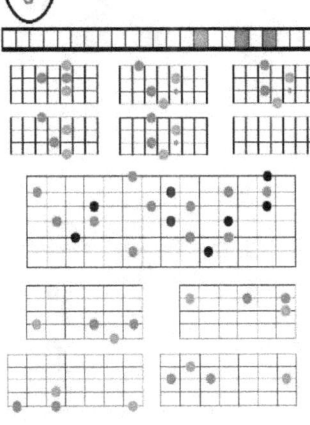
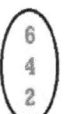
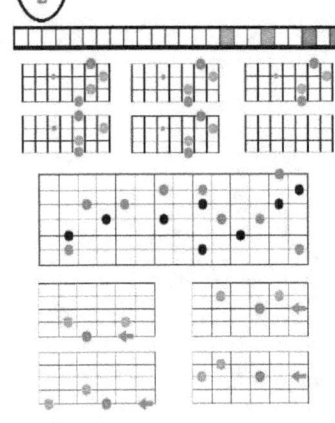

Full Diminished 7th

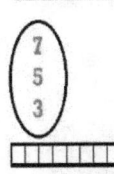
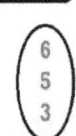
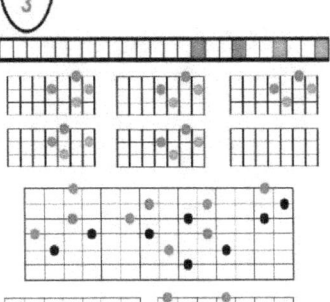
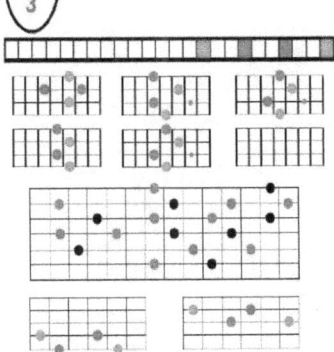
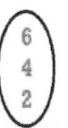
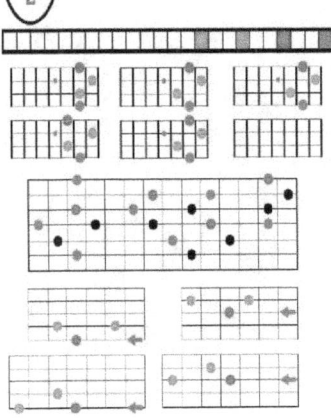

The pick ring

The image below is one of my inventions. I call this one pick ring, an active pick holder for playing various techniques in a guitar piece. With this tool, my picks do not lose anymore. Also, it allows me to use piking techniques, finger techniques and tow hand taping techniques at the same time. Moreover, this made of a ring and a spring and a clamp.

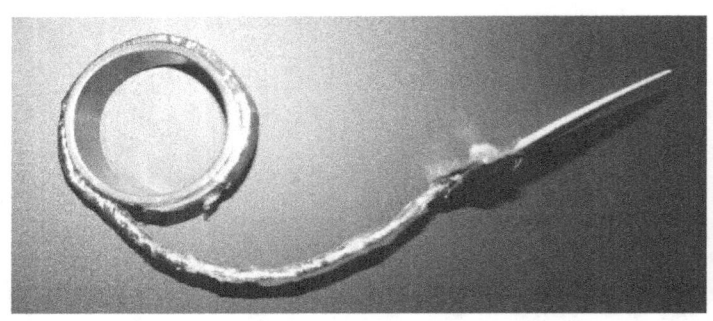
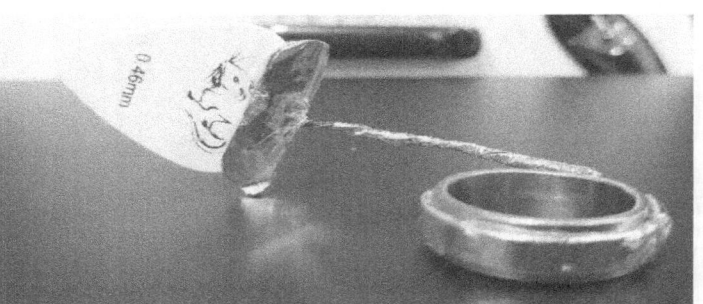

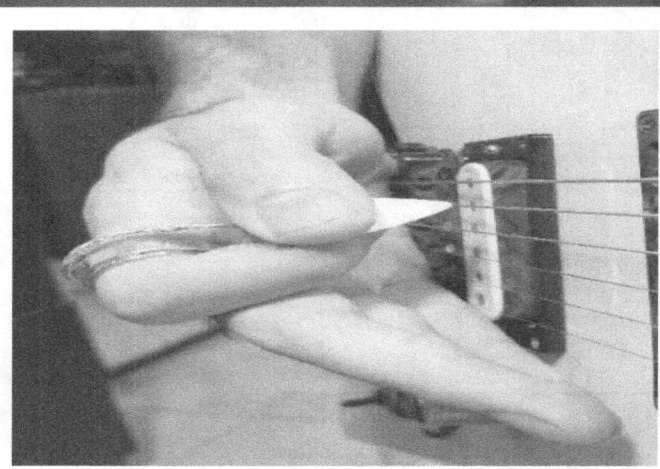
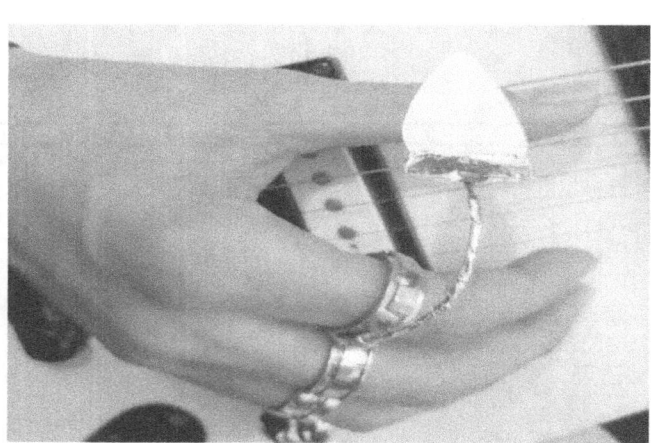
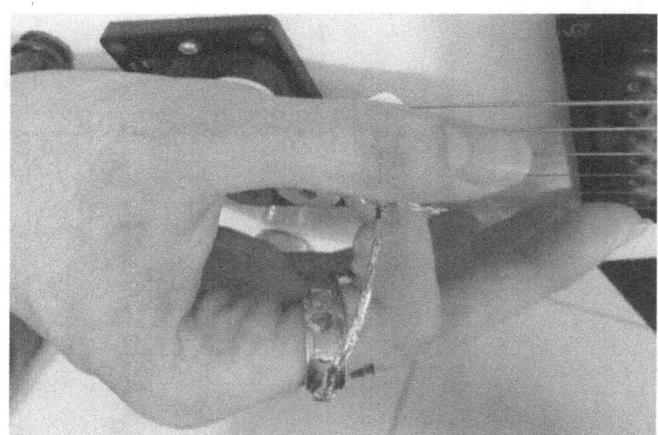

CHAPTER III
SPECIAL
PERFECTION
FOR
GUITARISTS

Professional modes and scales

All music in the world is one music, which is scattered among the cultures of the world's people. If we look deeply into the geographic music modes and scales, there are longitudinal and transverse relationships between them. Each geographic mode or scale has some parallel modes and scales from another geographical location. All of these modes and scales are matched together in the World Music Pyramid (chapter 4), and the result of these is the parallel harmonic revelations between the world modes of music. My innovative compositing method is a parallel-tonal compilation which is among the music of nations and peoples of the world. There are Harmonic relations among several world music modes and scales, Which allows the creation of parallel harmonics, Variable Harmony and Specific Spaces. This chapter is the introduction to the parallel-tonal music for guitarists also in this chapter there are many things for learning.

There are 12 scale and modes from around the world. They are very close together. Knowing them for any guitarist is required. These 12 modes Positioned for right-handed and left-handed guitarists. For each mode, there are several patterns in one octave, that have been written vertically. Also, they must be played from top to bottom, they are arranged. Each octave connects to the next octave. Finally, they combine and complete a full pattern in your mind. The reason for this method is to understand the positioning of the guitar for the student, in addition to the goals; Each pattern with its horizontal pattern (Which is, in fact, a different mode) have a near probability or a small difference. So recognizable with the eye, one translated note, one note added or deleted. This method classifies this 12 scale and modes mind.

On the next page, there is a complete map of modes and scales, and the next table is about the chords of the same modes and scales.

Church modes and their parallel modes

Row / Mode	Ionian	Dorian	Phrygian	Lydian	Mixolydian	Aeolian	Locrian
Hexatonic Blues	major blues	Blues tone note	SUSPENDED Hexa Blues	MAN GONG / MANGONG Hexa Blues	RITUSEN Hexa Blues	minor blues	
Pentatonic	MAJOR PENTATONIC	SUSPENDED PENTATONIC				MINOR PENTATONIC	
Heptatonic	Ionian	Dorian	Phrygian	Lydian	Mixolydian	Aeolian	Locrian
Harmonic minor	Ionian aug	Dorian #4	phrygian major	lydian #9		harmonic minor	locrian nat.6
○ **Double Harmonic Major** (Gypsy minor / HUNGARIAN MINOR)	IONIAN AUGMENTED #2		DHM Arabic Byzantine Gypsy major	LOCRIAN bb3 bb7	ULTRA PHRYGIAN HUNGARIAN MINOR Gypsy minor	ORIENTAL	IONIAN AUGMENTED #2
● **Harmonic Major**	harmonic major	dorian b5	phrygian b4	lydian b3	mixolydian b2	Lydian augmented	Phrygian #6
○ **Jazz Melodic minor**	Lydian augmented	Overtone scale	Mixolydian b6		Altered jazz minor scale	Altered jazz minor scale	SuperLocrian bb3
● **Double Harmonic Major**	DHM Arabic Byzantine Gypsy major	LYDIAN #2 #6	ULTRA PHRYGIAN HUNGARIAN MINOR Gypsy minor	ORIENTAL	IONIAN AUGMENTED #2	LOCRIAN bb3 bb7	
○ **Melodic Major**	Mixolydian b6	Locrian #2	Altered scale	lydian b3	Altered jazz minor scale	Lydian augmented	locrian bb7
Lydian Minor 4th Mode of Neapolitan Major	Neapolitan Major	Leading Whole-Tone	Augmented Lydian Dominan	LYDIAN MINOR	Major Locrian	SemiLocrian b4 (Altered Dominant Major bd3)	MIXOLYDIAN AUGMENTED
Neapolitan minor	Mixolydian b6	Locrian #2	IONIAN #2	ULTRA LOCRIAN bb3	NEAPOLITAN MINOR	LYDIAN #6	LOCRIAN bb3 bb7
Mela Rasikapriya HUNGARIAN GYPSY	Ioni MRP	Dori MRP	Phry MRP	Lydi MRP	Mixo MRP	Aeoli MRP	Locri MRP
(label row)		LOCRIAN DOMINANT					

Church modes and their parallel modes

Church modes and their parallel modes	Ionian	Dorian	Phrygian	Lydian	Mixolydian	Aeolian	Locrian
Hexatonic Blues	M6 m6	7sus2 7sus4	7sus4#5	M6♭5 M△7♭5	6sus2 6sus4	m7 dim°7 △7sus2	M7♭5
Pentatonic	M6 M△7	7sus2 7sus4	7sus4#5 △7sus4#5		6sus2 6sus4	m7	dim7
Heptatonic							
Harmonic minor	Aug△7	m7 m6 dim°7 7sus2 6sus2	M△7 M6 7sus4 6sus4	m△7 M7 Aug	dim°7 7sus2♭5 7sus4♭5 6sus2♭5 6sus4♭5	M7 M6 M6♭5 7sus4 6sus4♭5	Aug△7 dim°1
Harmonic Major	Aug△7	dim°7/ø7 7sus2♭5 sus4♭5 6sus2♭5 6sus4♭5	M7 M6 7sus2 6sus2	m△7 △7sus4 m△7 m7	M7 M6 Aug	m△7 dim°7 △7sus2	Aug△7 dim°1
Jazz Melodic minor	Aug△7 △7sus2 #5	m7 M7 m△7 m7 dim°7 dim°ø7	M△7 7sus2 7sus4	m△7 M7 △7sus4 m7	M7 M6	dim°7 △7sus2	m△7 △7sus2
Melodic Major	M△7 Aug△7 △7sus2 △7sus4	dim°7 Aug7	m△7 Aug	m△7 dim°7 △7sus2	m7 m6 △7sus4 6sus4	m△7 △7sus2	m△7 m7 dim°7
Double Harmonic Major	M△7	M7♭5	dim7	m△7 m7 △7sus2 7sus4	7sus2 △7sus4 6sus4	Aug△7 △7sus2 #5	Aug7 7sus2 #5 6
Double Harmonic minor	Aug△7	M7			M7♭5 M6♭5	Aug△7	M7♭5 6sus2♭5
Lydian Minor 4th Mode of Neapolitan Major	M7 △7sus2	M7♭5 △7sus4♭5	dim7	m△7 n7 △7sus2 7sus4	7sus2 △7sus4 6sus4	M△7 △7sus2 #5 7sus2	Aug7 7sus2 #5
Neapolitan minor	dim°7 7sus2	Aug7 7sus4 #5	m△7 m6 M△7M6 △7sus4 6sus6		m7 △7sus4 6sus4	M△7 m7 △7sus2	M△7 7sus4 #5
Neapolitan Major			Aug△7 Aug6		△7sus2 #5	M△7 △7sus2	Aug7 7sus4 #5
Mela Rasikapriya	m△7 dim △7sus2	7sus4 #5			6sus2♭5 6sus4♭5	M△7 m7 dim°7	M6 m6

PROFESSIONAL MODES AND SCALES FOR RIGHT-HANDS

Aeolian

Harmonic Minor
i	ii°	III+	iv	v
VI	vii°			

Aeolian
i	ii°	III	iv	v
VI	VII			

Minor Pentatonic
i	II6	iii 7/sus2	iv11	v sus2/4

Minor Blues
i 7/9/11	II7 ii7	IIIΔ7 5/6/9	iv7 +5/9/11	v6 sus2/4

Aeolian

bTR Ionian Aug #2				
I+	II₇	III	IV	v
vi	VII			

bTR Lydian Aug #2				
I+	ii°	III	iv°	v
vi	VII			

Jazz Minor				
i	II+	III	IV	v°
vi°	vii			

Minor Gypsy				
i	II	II+	IV₇	V
VI	vii			

Dorian

Dori MRP				
tonic 7sus4#5	II+Δ7/6 6sus2b5 6sus4b5	mediant	IV+Δ7 IVΔ7	VΔ7/7 v°7
VI6 vi6	vii° viiΔ7 Δ7sus2			

Locrian Dominant				
I+7	iiΔ7/6 IIΔ7/6 Δ7/6sus4	III+ sus2#5	ivΔ7 Δ7sus4	VΔ7/7 Δ7/7sus2
VI+7 7sus4#5	vii vii7/6 7sus2			

Leading Whole-Tone				
I7b5	ii°7	III7	iv6 6sus4	VΔ7/7 7sus2#5
VI+7	VII7 7sus2			

Locrian #2				
i°7	II+7	iiiΔ7/7 Δ7/7sus2/4	iv6/7 6/7sus4	V+Δ7 Δ7sus2#5
VI7/6 6/7sus2	VII+7 VII7 7sus2/4			

Dorian

bTR Lydian #2 #4				
I	ii	iii	IV	V+
VI₇	VII			

Dorian b5				
i°	ii	iii	IV	V+
vi°	VII			

Overtone				
I	ii°	iii°	iv	v
VI+	VII			

#TR Locrian bb3 bb7				
I₇	II	III	iv	v
VI	VII+			

Dorian

Dorian #4				
i	II	III	iv°	v
vi°	VII+			

Dorian				
i	ii	III	IV	v
vi°	VII			

Suspended Pentatonic				
i 7sus2	II /11	III sus2/4	iv	V₆

Suspended HB				
I 6/Δ7/9	ii +5/7/9/11	iii 6sus2/4	iv 7/11	V₇ v7
vi₆				

Lydian

#TR Lydi MRP				
tonic 6sus2b5 6sus4b5	II$_{\Delta 7}$ II$_{+\Delta 7}$	iii$_{\Delta 7/7}$ iii$_{+7}$	IV$_6$ iv$_6$	v$_{\Delta 7}$ v° Δ7sus2
Sub mediant 7sus4#5	VII$_{+\Delta 7/6}$			

#TR Ultra locrian				
I+ sus2#5	ii$_{\Delta 7}$ Δ7sus4	III$_{\Delta 7/7}$ Δ7/7sus2	IV$_{+7}$ 7sus4#5	V$_{6/7}$ 7sus2
VI$_{+7}$	vii$_{\Delta 7/6}$ VII$_{\Delta 7/6}$ Δ7/6sus4			

#TR Lydian Minor				
I$_{+7}$	ii$_6$ 6sus4	III$_{7/\Delta 7}$ 7sus2#5	IV$_{+7}$	V$_7$ 7sus2
VI$_{7b5}$	vii°$_7$			

Jazz Minor				
i$_{\Delta 7/7}$ Δ7/7sus2/4	ii$_{6/7}$ 6/7sus4	III$_{+\Delta 7}$ Δ7sus2#5	IV$_{7/6}$ 7/6sus2	V$_7$/V$_{+7}$ 7sus2/4
vi$_7$	VII+			

Lydian

Gipsy Minor				
i	II	III+	IV₇	V
VI	vii			

Lydian b3				
i	II	III+	iv°	V
vi°	vii			

#TR Locrian #2				
i°	ii	iii	IV+	V
VI	vii°			

Lydian #2 #6				
I	ii	iii	IV	V+
VI₇	VII			

Lydian

Lydian #9				
I	ii°	iii	iv°	V+
vi	VII			

Lydian				
I	II	iii	iv°	V
vi	vii			

Unknown				
I	ii sus2/4	iii	IV$_6$	V 7sus2

Unknown				
I	ii$_6$ sus2/4	iii 7/11	IV$_7$ iv7	V 6/Δ7/9
vi^{+5} 7/9/11				

Ionian

Ioni M R P

i△7 i° △7sus2	Super tonic 7sus4#5	III+△7/6	Sab dominant 6sus2b5 6sus4b5	V+△7 V△7
vi△7/7 vi°7	vii6 VII6			

Hungarian Gipsy

i7/6 i° 7sus2	II+7	iii△7/6 III△7/6 △7/6sus4	IV+ sus2#5	v△7 △7sus4
VI△7/7 △7/7sus2	VII△7/7 △7/7sus2			

Neapolitan Major

I7 7sus2	II7b5	iii°7	IV+7	v6 6sus4
VI+△7/7 7sus2#5	VII7			

Mixolydian b6

I7/I+7 7sus2/4	ii°7	III+7	iv△7/7 △7/7sus2/4	v7/6 7/6sus4
VI+△7 △7sus2#5	VII7/6 7/6sus2			

Ionian

Gipsy Major				
I	II	iii	iv	V
VI+	VII7			

Harmonic Major				
I	ii°	iii	iv	V
VI+	vii°			

Lydian Aug				
I	II	iii°	iv°	v
vi	VII+			

Ionian Aug #2				
I+	II7	III	IV	v
vi	VII			

Ionian

Ionian Aug				
I+	ii	III	IV	v°
vi	vii°			

Ionian				
I	ii	iii	IV	V
vi	vii°			

Major pentatonic				
I₆	ii 7sus2	III₁₁	IV sus2/4	v

Major Blues				
I₇ i₇	II 6/Δ7/9	iii+5 7/9/11	iv₆ sus2/4	v 7/11
vi₇				

Mixolydian

Mixo MRP

I+△7 / I△7	ii△7/7 / ii° 7	III6 / iii6	iv△7 / iv° / △7sus2	Dominant 7sus4#5
VI+△7/6 / Leading 6sus2b5 / 6sus4b5				

Neapolitan Minor

i△7 / △7sus4	II△7/7 / △7/7sus2	III+7 / 7sus4#5	iv° / iv6/7 / 7sus2	V+7
vi△7/6 / VI△7/7 / △7/7sus4	VII+ / sus2#5			

Major Locrian

i6 / 6sus4	II+△7/7 / 7sus2#5	III+7	IV7 / 7sus2	V7b5
vi7	VII+7			

Phrygian #6

i7/6 / 7/6sus4	II+△7 / △7sus2#5	III7/6 / 6/7sus2	IV7 / IV+7 / 7sus2/4	v° 7
VI+7	vii△7/7 / △7/7sus2/4			

Mixolydian

Oriental				
I	II+	III₇	IV	V
vi	vii			

Mixolydian b2				
I	II+	iii°	IV	v°
vi	vii			

#TR Altered				
i	ii	III+	IV	V
vi°	vii°			

#TR Ultra Phrygian				
i	ii	III	IV+	V₇
VI	VII			

Mixolydian

#TR Alt Dom bb7				
i°	ii	iii°	IV+	v
VI	VII			

Mixolydian				
I	ii	iii°	IV	v
vi	VII			

Ritusen				
i sus2/4	ii	III₆	iv 7sus2	v 11

Ritusen H B				
i₆ sus2/4	ii 7/11	III₇ iii₇	IV Δ7/6/9	v v+5 7/9/11

Phrygian

bTR Phry MRP				
I+Δ7/6	Supertonic 6sus2b5 6sus2b5	III+Δ7 IIIΔ7	ivΔ7/7 iv°7	V6 V6
vi viΔ7 Δ7sus2	Leading tone 7sus4#5			

bTR Ionian #2				
iΔ7/6 IΔ7/6 Δ7/6sus4	II+7 sus2#5	iiiΔ7 Δ7sus4	IVΔ7/7 Δ7/6sus2	V+7 7sus4#5
vi° vi 7sus2	VII+7			

Aug Lydian Dominan				
i°7	II+7	iii6 6sus4	IV+Δ7 7sus2#5	V+7
VI7 7sus2	VII7b5			

Altered				
I+7	iiΔ7/7 Δ7sus2/4	iii7/6 7/6sus4	IV+Δ7 sus2#5	V7/6 7/6sus2
VI+7 VI7 7sus2/4	vii°7			

Phrygian

Ultra Phrygian				
i	ii	III	IV+	V₇
VI	VII			

Phrygian b4				
i	ii	III	IV+	v°
VI	vii°			

Mixolydian b6				
i°	ii°	iii	iv	V+
VI	VII			

Gypsy Major				
I	II	iii	iv	V
VI+	VII₇			

Phrygian

Phrygian Major				
I	II	iii°	iv	v°
VI+	vii			

Phrygian				
i	II	III	iv	v°
VI	vii			

Mangong				
I₁₁	II sus2/4	iii	IV₆	V 7SUS2

Mangong H B					
I+ i₇/9/11	i+5 sus2/4	ii₆	iii₇/11	IV₇ iv₇	5/6/9

Locrian

Locrian MRP

I₆ i₆	iiⁱⁱΔ7 Δ7sus2	Mediant 7sus4#5	IV+Δ7/6	Dominant 6sus2b5 6sus4b5
VI+Δ7 VIΔ7	viiΔ7/7 vii°7			

bTR Mixolydian Aug

I+7 7sus4#5	ii ii 6/7 7sus2	III+7	ivΔ7/6 IVΔ2/6 Δ7/6sus4	V+ sus2#5
viΔ7 Δ7sus4	VIIΔ7/7 Δ7/7sus2			

bTR Super Locrian

I+7	II7 7sus2	III7b5	iv°7	V+7
vi₆ 6sus4	VII+Δ7 VII+7 7sus2#5			

bTR Overtone

I7/6 7/6SUS2	II7 II+7 7sus2/4	iii°7	IV+7	VΔ7/7 Δ7/7sus2/4
vi6/7 6/7sus4	VII+Δ7 Δ7sus2#5			

Locrian

Locrian bb3 bb7				
I₇	II	III	iv	v
VI	VII+			

Locrian bb7				
i°	II	iii°	iv	v
VI	VII+			

Phrygian #6				
I+	II	III	iv°	v°
vi	vii			

Oriental				
I	II+	III₇	IV	V
vi	vii			

Locrian

Locrian nat. 6				
i°	II+	iii	IV	V
vi°	vii			

Locrian				
i°	II	iii	iv	V
VI	vii			

Unknown				
i$_7$	II$_6$	iii sus2	IV$_{11}$	V sus2/4
vi				

Unknown				
i$_7$	II$_7$ / ii$_7$	III	iv$_{+5}$ 7/9/11	v$_6$ sus2/4
vi 7/11				

Other

Messiaen	MAm symmetrical	Diminished	Whole Tone

PROFESSIONAL MODES AND SCALES FOR LEFT-HANDS

Aeolian

bTR Aeoli MRP				
iΔ7/7 i$^*_7$	II$_6$ ii$_6$	iii iii$_{\Delta 7}$ Δ7sus2	Subdominant 7sus4#5	V+ Δ7/6
Submediant 6sus2b5 6sus4b5	VII+Δ7 VII$_{\Delta 7}$			

bTR Lydian #6				
I$_{\Delta 7/7}$ Δ7/7sus2	II$_{+7}$ 7sus4#5	iii iii$^*_{6/7}$ 7sus2	IV$_{+7}$	V$_{\Delta 7/6}$ V$_{\Delta 7/6}$ Δ7/6sus4
VI+ sus2#5	vii$_{\Delta 7}$ Δ7sus4			

bTR SemiLocrian b4				
I$_{+\Delta 7/7}$ 7sus2#5	II$_{+7}$	III$_7$ 7sus2	IV$_{7b5}$	v$^\circ_7$
VI$_{+7}$	vii$_6$ 6sus4			

bTR Lydian Aug				
I$_{+\Delta 7}$ 7sus2#5	II$_{6/7}$ 6/7sus2	III$_{+7}$ 7sus2/4	iv$^\circ_7$	V$_{+7}$
vi$_{\Delta 7/7}$ 7sus2/4 Δ7sus2/4	vii$_{6/7}$ 6/7sus4			

Aeolian

bTR Ionian Aug #2				
I+	II₇	III	IV	v
vi	VII			

bTR Lydian Aug #2				
I+	ii°	III	iv°	v
vi	VII			

Jazz Minor				
i	II+	III	IV	v°
vi°	vii			

Minor Gypsy				
i	II	II+	IV₇	V
VI	vii			

Aeolian

Harmonic Minor				
i	ii°	III+	iv	v
VI	vii°			

Aeolian				
i	ii°	III	iv	v
VI	VII			

Minor Pentatonic				
i	II6	iii 7/sus2	iv11	v sus2/4

Minor Blues				
i 7/9/11	II7 ii7	III△7 5/6/9	iv7 +5/9/11	v6 sus2/4

Dorian

Dori MRP				
tonic 7sus4#5	II+∆7/6	mediant 6sus2b5 6sus4b5	IV+∆7 IV∆7	V∆7/7 v°7
VI6 vi6	vii° vii∆7 ∆7sus2			

Locrian Dominant				
I+7	ii∆7/6 II∆7/6sus4	III+ sus2#5	iv∆7 ∆7sus4	V∆7/7 ∆7/7sus4
VI+7 7sus4#5	vii° vii7/6 7sus2			

Leading Whole-Tone				
I7b5	ii°7	III7	iv6 6sus4	V∆7/7 7sus2#5
VI+7	VII7 7sus2			

Locrian #2				
i°7	II+7	iii∆7/7 ∆7/7sus2/4	iv6/7 6/7sus4	V+∆7 ∆7sus2#5
VI7/6 6/7sus2	VII+7 VII7 7sus2/4			

Dorian

bTR Lydian #2 #4				
I	ii	iii	IV	V+
VI₇	VII			

Dorian b5				
i°	ii	iii	IV	V+
vi°	VII			

Overtone				
I	ii°	iii°	iv	v
VI+	VII			

#TR Locrian bb3 bb7				
I₇	II	III	iv	v
VI	VII+			

Dorian

Dorian #4				
i	II	III	iv°	v
vi°	VII+			

Dorian				
i	ii	III	IV	v
vi°	VII			

Suspended Pentatonic				
i 7sus2	II/11	III sus2/4	iv	V₆

Suspended HB				
I 6/Δ7/9	ii +5/7/9/11	iii 6sus2/4	iv 7/11	V₇ v7
vi₆				

Lydian

#TR Lydi MRP				
tonic 6sus2b5 6sus4b5	II△7 II+△7	iii△7/7 iii+7	IV6 iv6	v△7 v° △7sus2
Sub mediant 7sus4#5	VII+△7/6			

#TR Ultra locrian				
I+ sus2#5	ii△7 △7sus4	III△7/7 △7/7sus2	IV+7 7sus4#5	v6/7 7sus2
VI+7	vii△7/6 VII△7/6 △7/6sus4			

#TR Lydian Minor				
I+7	ii6 6sus4	III7/△7 7sus2#5	IV+7	V7 7sus2
VI7b5	vii°7			

Jazz Minor				
i△7/7 △7/7sus2	ii6/7 6/7sus4	III+△7 △7sus2#5	IV7/6 7/6sus2	V7/V+7 7sus2/4
vi7	VII+			

Lydian

Gipsy Minor				
i	II	III+	IV₇	V
VI	vii			

Lydian b3				
i	II	III+	iv°	V
vi°	vii			

#TR Locrian #2				
i°	ii	iii	IV+	V
VI	vii°			

Lydian #2 #6				
I	ii	iii	IV	V+
VI₇	VII			

Lydian

Lydian #9				
I	ii°	iii	iv°	V+
vi	VII			

Lydian				
I	II	iii	iv°	V
vi	vii			

Unknown				
I	ii sus2/4	iii	IV₆	V 7sus2

Unknown				
I	ii₆ sus2/4	iii 7/11	IV₇ iv7	V 6/△7/9
vi⁺⁵ 7/9/11				

Ionian

Ioni M R P

$i_{\Delta 7}$ $\Delta 7sus2$	$i°$ Super tonic $7sus4\#5$	$III+_{\Delta 7/6}$	Sub dominant $6sus2b5$ $6sus4b5$	$V+_{\Delta 7}$ $V_{\Delta 7}$
$vi_{\Delta 7/7}$ $vi°_7$	vii_6 VII_6			

Hungarian Gipsy

$i_{7/6}$ $7sus2$	$i°$ $II+_7$	$iii_{\Delta 7/6}$ $III_{\Delta 7/6}$ $\Delta 7/6sus4$	$IV+$ $sus2\#5$	$v_{\Delta 7}$ $\Delta 7sus4$
$VI_{\Delta 7/7}$ $\Delta 7/sus2$	$VII_{\Delta 7/7}$ $\Delta 7/sus2$			

Neapolitan Major

I_7 $7sus2$	II_{7b5}	$iii°_7$	$IV+_7$	v_6 $6sus4$
$VI+_{\Delta 7/7}$ $7sus2\#5$	VII_7			

Mixolydian b6

$I_{7/I+7}$ $7sus2/4$	$ii°_7$	$III+_7$	$iv_{\Delta 7/7}$ $\Delta 7/sus2/4$	$V_{7/6}$ $7/6sus4$
$VI+_{\Delta 7}$ $\Delta 7sus2\#5$	$VII_{7/6}$ $7/6sus2$			

Ionian

Gipsy Major
I	II	iii	iv	V
VI+	VII₇			

Harmonic Major
I	ii°	iii	iv	V
VI+	vii°			

Lydian Aug
I	II	iii°	iv°	v
vi	VII+			

Ionian Aug #2
I+	II₇	III	IV	v
vi	VII			

Ionian

Ionian Aug				
I+	ii	III	IV	v°
vi	vii°			

Ionian				
I	ii	iii	IV	V
vi	vii°			

Major pentatonic				
I₆	ii 7sus2	III₁₁	IV sus2/4	v

Major Blues				
I₇ / i₇	II 6/△7/9	iii+5 7/9/11	iv₆ sus2/4	v 7/11
vi₇				

Mixolydian

Mixo MRP

I+△7 / I△7	ii△7/7 / ii7	III6 / iii6	iv△7 / iv° / △7sus2	Dominant 7sus4#5
VI+△7/6	Leading 6sus2b5 6sus4b5			

Neapolitan Minor

i△7 / △7sus4	II△7/7 / △7/7sus2	III+7 / 7sus4#5	iv / iv6/7 / 7sus2	V+7
VI△7/6 / VII△7/7 / △7/7sus4	VII+ / sus2#5			

Major Locrian

i6 / 6sus4	II+△7 / 7sus2#5	III+7	IV7 / 6/7 / 7sus2	V7b5
vi7	VII+7			

Phrygian #6

i7/6 / 7/6sus4	II+△7 / △7sus2#5	III7/6 / 6/7sus2	IV7 / IV+7 / 7sus2/4	v°7
VI+7	vii△7/7 / △7/7sus2/4			

Mixolydian

Oriental				
I	II+	III₇	IV	V
vi	vii			

Mixolydian b2				
I	II+	iii°	IV	v°
vi	vii			

#TR Altered				
i	ii	III+	IV	V
vi°	vii°			

#TR Ultra Phrygian				
i	ii	III	IV+	V₇
VI	VII			

Mixolydian

#TR Alt Dom bb7				
i°	ii	iii°	IV+	v
VI	VII			

Mixolydian				
I	ii	iii°	IV	v
vi	VII			

Ritusen				
i sus2/4	ii	III₆	iv 7sus2	v 11

Ritusen H B				
i₆ sus2/4	ii 7/11	III₇ / iii₇	IV Δ7/6/9	v v+5 7/9/11

Phrygian

bTR Phry MRP				
I+Δ7/6	Supertonic 6sus2b5 6sus2b5	III+Δ7 IIIΔ7	ivΔ7/7 iv°7	V6 V6
vi°Δ7 Δ7sus2	Leading tone 7sus4#5			

bTR Ionian #2				
iΔ7/6 IΔ7/6 Δ7/6sus4	II+7 sus2#5	iiiΔ7 Δ7sus4	IVΔ7/7 Δ7/6sus2	V+7 7sus4#5
vi°Δ7/6 7sus2	VII+7			

Aug Lydian Dominan				
i°7	II+7	iii6 6sus4	IV+Δ7/7 7sus2#5	V+7
VI7 7sus2	VII7b5			

Altered				
I+7	iiΔ7/7 Δ7/7sus2/4	iii7/6 7/6sus4	IV+Δ7 Δ7sus2#5	V7/6 7/6sus2
VI+7 VI7 7sus2/4	vii°7			

Phrygian

Ultra Phrygian				
i	ii	III	IV+	V7
VI	VII			

Phrygian b4				
i	ii	III	IV+	v°
VI	vii°			

Mixolydian b6				
i°	ii°	iii	iv	V+
VI	VII			

Gypsy Major				
I	II	iii	iv	V
VI+	VII7			

Phrygian

Phrygian Major				
I	II	iii°	iv	v°
VI+	vii			

Phrygian				
i	II	III	iv	v°
VI	vii			

Mangong				
I₁₁	II sus2/4	iii	IV₆	V 7SUS2

Mangong H B					
I+ i₇/9/11	i+5 sus2/4	ii₆	iii₇/11	IV₇ iv₇	5/6/9

Locrian

Locrian MRP

I₆ i₆	ii ii°∆7	Mediant	IV +∆7/6	Dominant 6sus2b5
VI+∆7 VI∆7	vii∆7/7 vii°₇	∆7sus2	7sus4#5		6sus4b5

bTR Mixolydian Aug

I+₇ 7sus4#5	ii ii°₆/₇ 7sus2	III+₇	iv ∆7/6 IV ∆7/6 ∆7/6sus4	V+ sus2#5
vi ∆7 ∆7sus4	VII ∆7/7 ∆7/7sus2			

bTR Super Locrian

I+₇	II₇ 7sus2	III 7b5	iv°₇	V+₇
vi₆ 6sus4	VII+∆7 VII+₇ 7sus2#5			

bTR Overtone

I 7/6 7/6SUS2	II₇ II+₇ 7sus2/4	iii°₇	IV+₇	V∆7/7 ∆7/7sus2/4
vi 6/7 6/7sus4	VII+∆7 ∆7sus2#5			

Locrian

Locrian bb3 bb7				
I₇	II	III	iv	v
VI	VII+			

Locrian bb7				
i°	II	iii°	iv	v
VI	VII+			

Phrygian #6				
I+	II	III	iv°	v°
vi	vii			

Oriental				
I	II+	III₇	IV	V
vi	vii			

Locrian

Locrian nat. 6				
i°	II+	iii	IV	V
vi°	vii			

Locrian				
i°	II	iii	iv	V
VI	vii			

Unknown				
i7	II6	iii sus2	IV11	V sus2/4
vi				

Unknown				
i7	II7 / ii7	III	iv+5 7/9/11	v6 sus2/4
vi 7/11				

Other

Messiaen | MAm symmetrical | Diminished | Whole Tone

CHAPTER IV
THE WORLD
MUSIC
PYRAMID

How the pyramid works

The world music pyramid is a Multifunctional System for Music training, Understanding the music theory, recognizing other dimensions of music and it is a composition system for creating Parallel-tonal music. My innovative system for creating music Longitudinal and the transverse combination of all world music modes. The world modes and scales of all people, and relatives, and the races of the earth. All their modes and their names, and Connections of modes and harmonies Like a chain in a functional table. It works in different ways to create multi-tonal Compositions, with Special and traditional Harmonization and melodies.

The pyramid consists of two faces. The page on the left side is Pyramid, The place of the World Music Modes. Moreover, the Page on the right side is the Prism, Harmonization for the modes. Harmonies have longitudinal and transverse relationships. With this prism, we can make Parallel-tonal music. So start a Harmonic journey beyond the Cultures of the earth, and nations of the world and Human history.

Let's start the Harmonic journey. Consider the parallel worlds, imagine each mode and scale as a parallel world. They act in parallel movements. Imagine a piece of tonal music, All Harmonies are closed, and the rules of harmony dominate it. However, in fact of the universe, the same piece of music with the same rules in another mode or scale, it is implemented with the rules of harmonics.

Our ears and the rules of aesthetics discover and enforce these rules. Like the harmonic rules At times of the music history, But the art of music itself is more profound than our perception. Music is composed of contradictions Silence and Sound, Consonance and Dissonance, the intensity of sound, tempo (Fast and slow) and Frequency Response Music is broader than just hearing.

I believe that the world has been started with music. When I look at the stars, I see music pieces in them. The beauty of cosmic That Regular, texture of stars of the galaxies, and star rhythm patterns shining like that music we heard, really that have the universe is created by music. Everything in the universe has a frequency. If you look at the tables in this section (pyramid and prism), there are 12 horizontal blocks. We said that the octave was divided into 12 parts. each block is a tone of 12 tones in one octave. Also, where there is something written in the blocks means, there is a note on it. You will see a chain of notes in the horizontal blocks that the modes of the scales are there. Horizontal blocks only read from left to right, and Indicate the Degrees of each mode and scales, and intervals, that horizontal block have. If you read the pyramid from right to left, we have inverse modes of the mode.

Each note inside the pyramid means that there is a mode there. It may not be named, or unknown, or not used in music. However, in reality, these modes exist. I call them a circle of degree meaning; there are longitudinal and longitudinal expectations, with the other circle of degree is there. So either a mode or scale is there Inside the pyramid, Circle of degree can be a note, a mode or scale, also a set of intervals. The concept of the Circle of degree is an empty pattern or location for frequencies.

This symbol is the circle of degree.

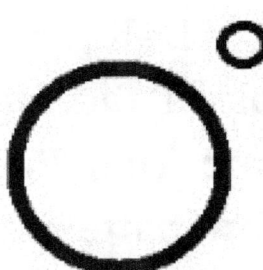

Moreover, this one is a circle of degree, with a 4 Point Star inside the circle. That manse a Quarter tone (50 cents higher) added to the note. This is an ornamental effect that becomes more authentic with the native music of the world. So with this effect, the scale and modes are sounding original.

+50 cent

it bent up

Everything is in sync with each other. There are also vertical blocks. When there is a circle of degrees in vertical blocks, that means; there is a parallel Relation between modes which can make a parallel harmonic motion between modes. So with this parallel motion on the scales and modes notes, we can have a wider range of harmony in music. The pyramid is on the left page, and the Prism is on the right page. Prism includes chords of the pyramid. Modes and scales of the pyramid are harmonized in Prism and are in the same horizontal blocks in the Prism if you look at the blocks of Prism. Within the blocks, chords and intervals have been abbreviated. Within the blocks, chords and intervals are written there. Maybe several types of chords and intervals in a circle of degrees except. Chords are made up of combinations of intervals; there may be several types of chords and intervals in a circle of degrees.

Chords are made up of combinations of intervals. In every circle of degrees, I put the most straightforward chords can be possible, with the order. I did not write extended chords in a circle of degrees, because other harmonies were ignored and forgotten. Moreover, parallel harmonic communication between longitudinal blocks was unobtrusive. You can use Extended Chords If you want with a simple mental calculation. Just look at the chords inside the circle of degree, Put the intervals together, and use the extended chords would you like.

In each block, several charts have been abbreviated, for example; The Phrase M 6/7/Δ7 means M6 & M7 & MΔ7. or this phrase 6/7/Δ7 SUS 2/4 means 6sus2 & 6sus4 & 7sus2 & 7sus4 & Δ7sus2 & Δ7sus4. To create Parallel Harmony, look at the vertical blocks in the Prism. In the longitudinal equilibrium of circle of degrees Chords and intervals, that are repeated; are the Gates of creating parallel harmonies. Furthermore, that vertical circle of degrees has more the same chords and intervals. They are better for making Parallel Harmonies. This parallel harmonic movement can possible in all chords of a parallel harmonic song.

On the other hand, the song can move, between scale and modes of the world. The world music pyramid is compatible with all music of the world, and history.

Everything about humanity and world music is in this chapter. Finally, there are 15 Persians modes, that I had to develop them from traditional Persian music, with Combining 4 Tetrachords of Persian Music. And analysis the 12th Maqams of the ancient and ethnic music of Iran. I designed these 15 modes Persian modes are close to the world music and have scattered connections. Persian music simplification and clarification for all the musicians of the world, they can be understood and Performing. I also devised Persian chords to harmonize these Persian modes. For all the years of my life, I have to understand the relationship between traditional music nations and connect cultures.

By placing each scale in this table, you will have the scale in different tones. Each horizontal icon is a chromatic scale; therefore, each circle of degree can run on every tone.

A	Bb/A#	B	C	Db/C#	D	Eb/D#	E	F	Gb/F#	G	Ab/G#	A
Bb/A#	B	C	Db/C#	D	Eb/D#	E	F	Gb/F#	G	Ab/G#	A	Bb/A#
B	C	Db/C#	D	Eb/D#	E	F	Gb/F#	G	Ab/G#	A	Bb/A#	B
C	Db/C#	D	Eb/D#	E	F	Gb/F#	G	Ab/G#	A	Bb/A#	B	C
Db/C#	D	Eb/D#	E	F	Gb/F#	G	Ab/G#	A	Bb/A#	B	C	Db/C#
D	Eb/D#	E	F	Gb/F#	G	Ab/G#	A	Bb/A#	B	C	Db/C#	D
Eb/D#	E	F	Gb/F#	G	Ab/G#	A	Bb/A#	B	C	Db/C#	D	Eb/D#
E	F	Gb/F#	G	Ab/G#	A	Bb/A#	B	C	Db/C#	D	Eb/D#	E
F	Gb/F#	G	Ab/G#	A	Bb/A#	B	C	Db/C#	D	Eb/D#	E	F
Gb/F#	G	Ab/G#	A	Bb/A#	B	C	Db/C#	D	Eb/D#	E	F	Gb/F#
G	Ab/G#	A	Bb/A#	B	C	Db/C#	D	Eb/D#	E	F	Gb/F#	G
Ab/G#	A	Bb/A#	B	C	Db/C#	D	Eb/D#	E	F	Gb/F#	G	Ab/G#
A	Bb/A#	B	C	Db/C#	D	Eb/D#	E	F	Gb/F#	G	Ab/G#	A

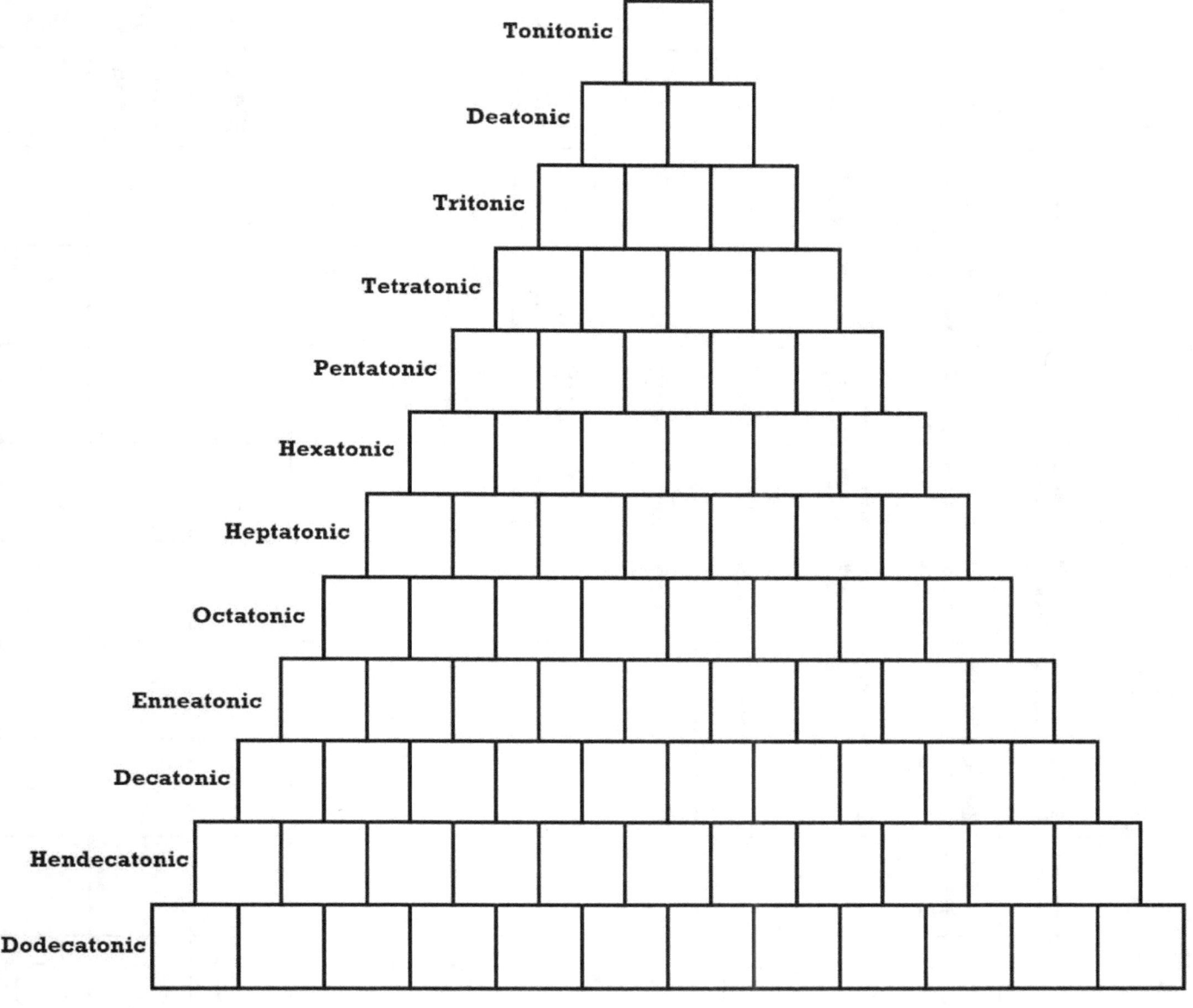

1_**Tonitonic** (tone root note) (unisun interval & octave interval)
2_**Deatonic** (melodic intervals & harmonic intervals)
3_**Tritonic (Triads)**
4_**Tetratonic (7th chords)**
5_**Pentatonic**
6_**Hexatonic**
7_**Heptatonic**
8_**Octatonic**
9_**Enneatonic (Nonatonic)**
10_**Decatonic**
11_**Hendecatonic**
12_**Dodecatonic (Chromatic)**

Chromatic dodeca tonic	II	III	IV	V	VI	VII	VIII	IX	X	XI	XII
Chromatic undeca mirror	II	III	IV	V	VI	VII	VIII	IX	X	XI	
Chromatic deca mirror	II	III	IV	V	VI	VII	VIII	IX	X		
Chromatic ennea mirror	II	III	IV	V	VI	VII	VIII	IX			
Chromatic octa mirror	II	III	IV	V	VI	VII	VIII				
Chromatic hepta mirror	II	III	IV	V	VI	VII					
Chromatic hexa mirror	II	III	IV	V	VI						
Chromatic penta mirror	II	III	IV	V							
Chromatic tetra mirror	II	III	IV								
Chromatic tri mirror	II	III									
Major minor mixed		○	○	○	minor pentatonic with leading tones		○	○	○	○	○
Full minor		○	○	Blues ennea tonic		○	○	○	Chromatic bebop	○	
○	Kiourdi		○	○		○	○	○	○	○	
+50 cent ⊕ it bent up		○	○	+50 cent ⊕ it bent up		○ +50 cent ⊕ it bent up	○	○	+50 cent ⊕ it bent up	Maqam zirafkand	
Major minor mixed		○	○	○	minor pentatonic with leading tones		○	○	○	○	○
	Messiaen mode 7	○	○	○		○	○	○	Messiaen mode 7 inverse	Messiaen mode 7 inverse	

The earth culture music rainbow

Chromatic dodeca tonic	II	III	IV	V	VI	VII	VIII	IX	X	XI	XII
	XI	X	IX	VIII	VII	VI	V	IV	III	II	Chromatic undeca mirror
		X	IX	VIII	VII	VI	V	IV	III	II	Chromatic deca mirror
			IX	VIII	VII	VI	V	IV	III	II	Chromatic ennea mirror
				VIII	VII	VI	V	IV	III	II	Chromatic octa mirror
					VII	VI	V	IV	III	II	Chromatic hepta mirror
						VI	V	IV	III	II	Chromatic hexa mirror
							V	IV	III	II	Chromatic penta mirror
								IV	III	II	Chromatic tetra mirror
									III	II	Chromatic tri mirror
M 6/7/△7 m 6/7/△7 + 7/△7 6/7/△7 SUS 2/4		m 6/7 o7 o7 6/7 SUS 2/4	M 6/△7 +△7 6/△7 SUS 2/4	M/m 7/△7 ø 7/△7 7/△7 SUS 2/4	M 6/7/△7 m 6/7 + 7/△7 6/7/△7 SUS 2/4		M 6/7 m 6/7 + 7 6/7 SUS 2/4	M 6/△7 m 6/△7 +△7 o7/△7 6/△7 SUS 2	m 7/△7 ø 7/△7 7/△7 SUS 2/4	M 6/7/△7 6/7/△7 SUS 2	+ 7/△7 o7 o7 o△7 (add 11)
m 6/7/△7 6/7/△7 SUS 2/4		m 6/7/△7 o7 o7 o△7 6/7/△7 SUS 4	M 6/△7 +△7 6/△7 SUS 4		M 6/7/△7 m 6/7 o7 o7 6/7/ SUS 2/4		M 7 m 7 + 7 7 SUS 2/4	M 6/△7 m 6/△7 o 7/△7 6/△7 SUS 2	ø 7/△7 (add 9) (add 11)	M 6/7/△7 6/7/△7 SUS 2	+ 7/△7 o7 o7 o△7
M 6/7/△7 + 7/△7 6/7/△7 SUS 2/4		m 6/7 o7 o7 6/7/ SUS 2/4		M/m 7 + 7 o7 7 SUS 4	M 6/△7 m 6/△7 o 7/△7 6/△7 SUS 2/4		M 6/7 m 6/7 6/7 SUS 2/4	+△7 oØ7 Mb5 △7 m#5 △7	m 7/△7 7/△7 SUS 2/4	M 6/7/△7 6/7/△7 SUS 2	o7 o7 o△7
(1°)/(7°) M(1°) 6/(7°)/△7 +(1°) (7°)/△7 6/(7°)/△7 SUS(1°) 2 6/(7°)/△7 SUS(1°) 4		(3°)/(7°) m(3°) 6/(7°)/△7 o(3°)/ (7°) ø(3°) 7 6/(7°) SUS 2/4		M/m 7 +(5°) 7 ø(3°)(5°) 7 ø(5°) 7 7 SUS 4	M(1°)(5°) 6/△7 m(1°)(5°) 6/△7 o 7/△7 6/△7 SUS 2(2°)(5°) 6/△7 SUS 4(4°)(5°)		M 6/7/(7°) m(3°) 6/7/(7°) 6/(7°)/ SUS 2 6/(7°)/ SUS 4(4°) also all can be (1°)	+(3°) △7 o7/ (7°) M(3°)b5 △7 m#5 △7	m(3°) 7/(7°)/△7 7/(7°)/△7 SUS 4	M(1°)(5°) 6(6°)/7/△7 7/(7°)/△7 SUS 2 (1°)(2°)(5°)	o(5°)7 ø(5°)7 o(5°)/△7
M 6/7/△7 m 6/7/△7 + 7/△7 6/7/△7 SUS 2/4		m 6/7 o7 o7 6/7/ SUS 2/4	M 6/△7 +△7 6/△7 SUS 2/4	M/m 7/△7 + 7/△7 ø 7/△7 7/△7 SUS 2/4	M 6/7/△7 m 6/7 + 7/△7 6/7/△7 SUS 2/4		M 6/7 m 6/7 + 7 6/7 SUS 2/4	M 6/△7 m 6/△7 +△7 o7/△7 6/△7 SUS 2	m 7/△7 ø 7/△7 7/△7 SUS 2/4	M 6/7/△7 6/7/△7 SUS 2	+ 7/△7 o7 o7 o△7 (add 11)
	M 6/7 m 6/7 + 7 o7 o7 6/7 SUS 2/4	m 6/△7 o 7/△7 6/△7 SUS 2/4	M 7/△7 +△7 7/△7 SUS 2/4	M 6/7/△7 m 7/△7 o7 o7 o△7 6/7/△7 SUS 2/4	+ 7/△7 Mb5 6/7/△7 m#5 6/7/△7 (add 9 & 11)		M 6/7 m 6/7 + 7 o7 o7 6/7 SUS 2	m 6/△7 o 7/△7 6/△7 SUS 2	M 7/△7 + 7 7/△7 SUS 2/4	M 6/7/△7 o7 o7 o△7 6/7/△7 SUS 4	+ 7/△7 o7 o7 o△7 6/7/△7 SUS 2/4 b5 6/7/△7 SUS 2/4 #5

The earth culture music rainbow

											Messiaen mode 7	Messiaen mode 7 inverse
	Messiaen mode 7	○	○	○	○		○	○	○			○ inverse
		Untitled ennea tonic	○	○	○		○	○	○	○	○	○
	○		○	○	○		○	○	Symmetrical ennea tonic	○	○
	○	○		Untitled ennea tonic	○		○	○	○	○	○
	○		○	○	Untitled ennea tonic		○	○	○	○	○
	○		○	○			○	Harmonic neapolitan minor	○	○	○
	○		○	○				Untitled heptat tonic	○	○	○
	○			Mixo blues				○	○	○	○
	○		○	○			○	Harmonic neapolitan minor	○	○	○
		○	○	Blues variation			○	○	○	○	○
		○	○	○			○	○		Oriental	○
		○	○	Blues variation			○	○	○	○	○
	○	○	○	Untitled ennea tonic			○	○	○	○	○
	Chromatic diatonic dorian mixed	○	○	Taishikicho Lydian Mixolydian mixed		Houseini Major Pentatonic mixed		○	○	○	○
		○	○	Blues variation			○	○	○	○	○
		Messiaen mode 4	○	○	○			○	○	○	Messiaen mode 4 inverse

	M 6/7 m 6/7 + 7 o7 ø7 6/7 SUS 2	m 6/△7 ø 7/△7 6/△7 SUS 2/4	M 7/△7 + 7/△7 7/△7 SUS 2/4	M 6/7/△7 m 6/7/△7 o7 ø7 o△7 6/7/△7 SUS 2/4	+ 7/△7 o7 ø7 o△7 Mb5 6/7/△7 m♭5 6/7/△7 (add 9 & 11)		M 6/7 m 6/7 + 7 o7 ø7 6/7 SUS 2	m 6/△7 ø 7/△7 6/△7 SUS 2	M 7/△7 + 7/△7 7/△7 SUS 2/4	M 6/7/△7 m 6/7/△7 o7 ø7 o△7 6/7/△7 SUS 4	+ 7/△7 o7 ø7 o△7 6/7/△7 SUS 2/4 b5
		m 6 o 7 6 SUS 2/4	M △7 + △7 △7 SUS 2/4	M/m 7/△7 ø 7/△7 7/△7 SUS 2/4	o7 ø7 o△7 Mb5 6/7/△7 (add 9 & 11)		M 6/7 m 6/7 + 7 6/7 SUS 2	m 6/△7 o 7/△7 6/△7 SUS 2	7/△7 SUS 2/4	M 6/△7 6/7/△7 SUS 4	+ 7/△7 o7 ø7 o△7 Mb5 6/7/△7 m♭5 6/7/△7 6/7/△7 SUS 4 b5/#5
	M 6/7 m 6/7 + 7 o7 ø7 6/7 SUS 2		M 7 + 7 7 SUS 2/4	M/m 7/△7 ø 7/△7 7/△7 SUS 4	+ 7/△7 o7 ø7 Mb5 7/△7 m♯5 7/△7 (add 9 & 11)		+ 7 o7 ø7 Mb5 6/7 m♯5 6/7 6/7 SUS 2 b5/♯5	m 6/△7 6/△7 SUS 2/4	M 7/△7 + 7/△7 7/△7 SUS 2	m 6/7/△7 o7 ø7 o△7 6/7/△7 SUS 4	+ 7/△7 Mb5 6/7/△7 6/7/△7 SUS 2/4 ♯5
	M 6/7 m 6/7 + 7 o7 ø7	m 6/△7 o 7/△7 6/△7 SUS 2/4		M 6/7 m 6/7 o7 ø7 6/7 SUS 4	+ △7 o7 o△7 Mb5 6/△7 m♯5 6/△7 (add 9 & 11)	M 6/7 m 6/7 + 7 6/7 SUS 2		o7 ø7 m♯5 6/△7 6/△7 SUS 2/4 b5 6/△7 SUS 2/4 ♯5	M 7/△7 + 7/△7 7/△7 SUS 2/4	M 6/△7 m 6/7/△7 o7 ø7 o△7	o7 ø7 o△7 m♯5 6/7/△7 6/△7 SUS 2/4 b5 6/△7 SUS 2/4 ♯5
	M 6/7 m 6/7 + 7 o7 ø7 6/7 SUS 2		M 7 + 7 7 SUS 2/4	M/m 7/△7 ø 7/△7 7/△7 SUS 4	+ 7/△7 o7 ø7 Mb5 7/△7 m♯5 7/△7 (add 9 & 11)	+ 7 o7 ø7 Mb5 6/7 m♯5 6/7 6/7 SUS 2 b5/♯5		m 6/△7 6/△7 SUS 2	M 7/△7 + 7/△7 7/△7 SUS 2	m 6/7/△7 o7 ø7 o△7	+ 7/△7 Mb5 6/7/△7 6/7/△7 SUS 2/4 ♯5
	m 6/7 o7 ø7 6/7 SUS 2		M 7 + 7 7 SUS 4	M 6/7 m 6/△7 o 7/△7 6/△7 SUS 4			o7 6 SUS 2 Mb5 6 m♯5 6	m △7 △7 SUS 2/4	M 7/△7 7/△7 SUS 2	o7 ø7 o△7 6/7/△7 SUS 4 b5	+ 7/△7 (add 9 & 11)
	m 6/7 6/7 SUS 2		7 SUS 4	M 6/△7 6/△7 SUS 4				m SUS 4 M add 9 Mb5 △7	M △7 △7 SUS 2 M add 9 Mb5 △7	ø7 o△7 7/△7 SUS 4 b5	M no 5th 6/7/△7 M no 5th add 11
	m 6/7			M 6 6 SUS 4				m♯5 SUS 4 ♯5 m♯5 add 11	M △7 △7 SUS 2	ø7 o△7	△ (no 3 , no 5) △7/9/11/13 (no3,no5)
	m 6/7 o7 ø7 6/7 SUS 2		M 7 + 7 7 SUS 4	M 6/△7 m 6/△7 o 7/△7 6/△7 SUS 4			o7 6 SUS 2 Mb5 6 m♯5 6	m △7 △7 SUS 2/4	M 7/△7 7/△7 SUS 2	o7 ø7 o△7 6/7/△7 SUS 4 b5	+ 7/△7 (add 9 & 11)
		6 SUS 2/4	M △7 + △7 △7 SUS 4	M/m 7/△7 ø 7/△7 7/△7 SUS 4			M 6 m 6 + 6 SUS 2	m △7 o△7 △7 SUS 2	7/△7 SUS 4	Mb5 6/7/△7 6/7/△7 SUS 4 b5	m♯5 6/7/△7 6/7/△7 SUS 4 ♯5
		6 SUS 2/4 b5 6 SUS 2/4 ♯5	M △7 + △7 △7 SUS 4	M/m 7/△7 ø 7/△7			M 6 m 6 +	m △7 o△7 △7 SUS 2		Mb5 6/7 6/7 SUS 4 b5	m♯5 6/△7 6/△7 SUS 4 ♯5
		6 SUS 2/4	M △7 + △7 △7 SUS 4	M/m 7/△7 ø 7/△7 7/△7 SUS 4			M 6 m 6 + 6 SUS 2	m △7 o△7 △7 SUS 2	7/△7 SUS 4	Mb5 6/7/△7 6/7/△7 SUS 4 b5	m♯5 6/7/△7 6/7/△7 SUS 4 ♯5
	m 6/7 o7 ø7 6/7 SUS 2	7/△7 SUS 2/4	M 7/△7 + 7/△7 7/△7 SUS 4	M 6/7/△7 m 6/7/△7 o7 ø7 o△7 6/7/△7 SUS 4			M 6 m 6 + o7 6 SUS 2	m △7 o△7 △7 SUS 2/4	M 7/△7 7/△7 SUS 2/4	o7 ø7 o△7 Mb5 6/7/△7 6/7/△7 SUS 4 b5	+ 7/△7 m♯5 6/7/△7 6/7/△7 SUS 2/4 ♯5
	m 6/7 6/7 SUS 2/4	M 6/△7 + △7 △7 SUS 2	M 7/△7 o7 o△7 7/△7 SUS 4	M 6/7/△7 6/7/△7 SUS 2/4		M 6/7 m 6/7 + 7 6/7 SUS 2/4		m 7 o7 7 SUS 2/4	M 6/△7 6/△7 SUS 2/4	o7 o△7 Mb5 7/△7 m♯5 7/△7 6/7/△7 SUS 2/4 b5	M 6/7/△7 m 6/7/△7
		6 SUS 2/4	M △7 + △7 △7 SUS 4	M/m 7/△7 ø 7/△7			M 6 m 6 + 6 SUS 2	m △7 o△7 △7 SUS 2	7/△7 SUS 4	Mb5 6/7/△7 6/7/△7 SUS 4 b5	m♯5 6/7/△7 6/7/△7 SUS 4 ♯5
		m 6 o 7 6 SUS 2	△7 SUS 2/4	M 6/△7 7/△7 SUS 4	o7 ø7 o△7 Mb5 6/7/△7 6/7/△7 SUS 4 b5			m 6 o 7 6 SUS 2	△7 SUS 2/4	M 7/△7 7/△7 SUS 4	o7 ø7 o△7 Mb5 6/7/△7 6/7/△7 SUS 4 b5

		Messiaen mode 4	○	○	○			○	○	○	Messiaen mode 4 inverse
		○		○	○			○	○	○	○
	○	○		○	○			○	○	○	○
	○	Nine tone		Youlan	○	○		○	○	○	○
	○	○	○		○	○		○	○	Moorish phrygian *Phrygian double harmonic major mixed*	○
	○	Nine tone		Youlan	○	○		○	○	○	○
	○				○	○	○		○	○	Neveseri	○
	○				○		○		○	Chromatic phrygian inverse	○	○
	○	○		○		○		○	○	○	Raga miyan malhar
	Dorian Aeolian mixed		Phrygian Locrian mixed	Major Lydian *tchikostiano*		Bebop dorian Bebop minor		Phrygian Aeolian mixed	○	Prokofiev	Bebop dominant
	○		○	○				○	○	○	○
			○	○				○	Raga Vijayasri	○	○
			○	○		○		○	○	○	Raga Malkauns
		○		○		○		○	○	Enigmatic Major	○
	○			○		○		○	○	Enigmatic minor	○
	○		○			Untitled heptatonic		○	○	○	○

The earth culture music rainbow

		m 6 o 7 6 SUS 2	Δ7 SUS 2/4	M 7/Δ7 7/Δ7 SUS 4	o7 ø7 oΔ7 Mb5 6/7/Δ7 6/7/Δ7 SUS 4 b5			m 6 o 7 6 SUS 2	Δ7 SUS 2/4	M 7/Δ7 7/Δ7 SUS 4	o7 ø7 oΔ7 Mb5 6/7/Δ7 6/7/Δ7 SUS 4 b5
		m 6 o 7 6 SUS 2		M 7 7 SUS 4	o7 oΔ7 Mb5 6/Δ7 6/Δ7 SUS 4 b5			o 7 m#5 6 6 SUS 2 #5 6 SUS 2 b5	Δ7 SUS 2/4	M 7/Δ7	o7 ø7 oΔ7
	M 6/7 m 6/7 + 7	m 6/Δ7 o7 Δ7		M 6/7 6/7 SUS 4	o7 oΔ7 Mb5 6/Δ7 6/Δ7 SUS 4 b5/#5			o7 m#5 6 6 SUS 2/4 #5	M Δ7 + Δ7 Δ7 SUS 2/4	M/m 7/Δ7 ø 7/Δ7 7/Δ7 SUS 2/4	o7 ø7 oΔ7 6/7/Δ7 SUS 2 b5 6/7/Δ7 SUS 4 b5
	M 6/7 m 6/7 + 7 6/7 SUS 2/4	M 6/Δ7 m 6/Δ7 + Δ7 o 7/Δ7 6/Δ7 SUS 2		M 6/7 6/7 SUS 2/4	+ Δ7 o7 oΔ7 Mb5 6/Δ7 m#5 6/Δ7 6/Δ7 SUS 2/4 b5 6/Δ7 SUS 2/4 #5	M/m 7/Δ7 + 7/Δ7 7/Δ7 SUS 2/4		m#5 6/7 6/7 SUS 2/4 #5	M Δ7 + Δ7 Δ7 SUS 2/4	M/m 7/Δ7 + 7/Δ7 ø 7/Δ7 7/Δ7 SUS 2/4	m 6/7/Δ7 o7 ø7 oΔ7 6/7/Δ7 SUS 2/4
	M 6/7 + 7 6/7 SUS 2/4	M 6/Δ7 m 6/Δ7 + Δ7 o 7/Δ7	m 7/Δ7 ø 7/Δ7 7/Δ7 SUS 2/4		+ 7 o7 ø7 m#5 7	M 6/Δ7 m 6/Δ7 + Δ7 6/Δ7 SUS 2/4		m 6/7 o7 ø7 6/7 SUS 2/4	+ 7 Mb5 6/Δ7 6/Δ7 SUS 2/4 b5 6/Δ7 SUS 2/4 #5	M/m 7/Δ7 + 7/Δ7 7/Δ7 SUS 4	M 6/7/Δ7 m 6/7/Δ7 o7 ø7 oΔ7 6/7/Δ7 SUS 2
	M 6/7 m 6/7 + 7 6/7 SUS 2/4	M 6/Δ7 m 6/Δ7 + Δ7 o 7/Δ7 6/Δ7 SUS 2		M 6/7 6/7 SUS 2/4	+ Δ7 o7 oΔ7 Mb5 6/Δ7 m#5 6/Δ7 6/Δ7 SUS 2/4 #5	M/m 7/Δ7 + 7/Δ7 7/Δ7 SUS 2/4		m#5 6/7 6/7 SUS 2/4 #5	M Δ7 + Δ7 Δ7 SUS 2/4	M/m 7/Δ7 + 7/Δ7 ø 7/Δ7 7/Δ7 SUS 2/4	m 6/7/Δ7 o7 ø7 oΔ7 6/7/Δ7 SUS 2/4
	M 6/7 m 6/7 + 7 6/7 SUS 4			M 6 6 SUS 2/4	+ Δ7 oΔ7 Mb5 Δ7 m#5 Δ7 Δ7 SUS 4 b5 Δ7 SUS 4 #5	M/m 7/Δ7 7/Δ7 SUS 2/4		m#5 6/7 6/7 SUS 2/4 #5	M 6/Δ7 + Δ7 6/Δ7 SUS 2	m 7/Δ7 ø 7/Δ7	6/7/Δ7 SUS 2/4
	m 6/7 + 7 6/7 SUS 4			M 6 6 SUS 2/4		M/m 7 7 SUS 2/4		m#5 7 7 SUS 4 #5	M 6/Δ7 6/Δ7 SUS 2	ø 7/Δ7 m#5 7/Δ7	6/7/Δ7 SUS 2/4
	m 6/7 6/7 SUS 4	M 6/Δ7 + Δ7 6/Δ7 SUS 2		M 6/7 6/7 SUS 2/4		M/m 7 + 7 7 SUS 2/4		ø7 m#5 7 7 SUS 2/4 b5 7 SUS 2/4 #5	M 6/Δ7 6/Δ7 SUS 2	+ 7/Δ7 o7 oΔ7 Mb5 7/Δ7 m#5 7/Δ7	m 6/7/Δ7 6/7/Δ7 SUS 2/4
	m 6/7 6/7 SUS 2/4	M 6/Δ7 + Δ7 6/Δ7 SUS 2	m 7 ø 7 7 SUS 4	M 6/7 6/7 SUS 2/4		M/m 6/7 6/7 SUS 2/4		m 7 7 SUS 2/4	M 6/Δ7 6/Δ7 SUS 2	o7 oΔ7 m#5 7/Δ7 7/Δ7 SUS 4 b5 7/Δ7 SUS 4 #5	M 6/7/Δ7 6/7/Δ7 SUS 2/4
	m 6/7 6/7 SUS 2		7 SUS 4	M 6/7 6/7 SUS 4				m SUS 2/4	M Δ7 Δ7 SUS 2	o7 oΔ7 7/Δ7 SUS 4 b5	M(no 5) 6/7/Δ7 M(no 5) add 9 M(no 5) add 11
			SUS 4	M Δ7				m SUS 2/4		Δ7 SUS 2	7/Δ7 SUS 4 b5	M(no 5) 6/7/Δ7
			m SUS 4	M SUS 2/4		M(no 5) 6/7 m(no 5) 6/7 6/7 SUS 2(no 5) 6/7 SUS 4(no 5)		M 7 7 SUS 2	6/Δ7 SUS 2	7/Δ7 SUS 4 b5 7/Δ7 SUS 4 #5	M 6/7/Δ7 6/7/Δ7 SUS 4
		M 6 + 6 SUS 2		M 7 7 SUS 2/4		+ 7 m#5 7 7 SUS 2/4 #5		ø7 m#5 7 7 SUS 2 b5 7 SUS 2 #5	6/Δ7 SUS 2	+ 7/Δ7 Mb5 7/Δ7	m 6/7/Δ7 6/7/Δ7 SUS 4
	m 6/7/Δ7 6/7 SUS 4			M 6 6 SUS 2/4		M 7 m 7 7 SUS 2/4		m#5 7 7 SUS 2/4 #5	M 6/Δ7 6/Δ7 SUS 2	o7 oΔ7 m#5 7/Δ7	6/7/Δ7 SUS 2/4
	6 SUS 2 7 SUS 2 6 SUS 4 7 SUS 4		m 6 ø7 6 SUS 4			M 6 m 6 6 SUS 2/4		m 7 7 SUS 2/4	Mb5 6/Δ7 6/Δ7 SUS 2 b5	m#5 7/Δ7 7/Δ7 SUS 4	M 6/7/Δ7 6/7/Δ7 SUS 2

The earth culture music rainbow

						Untitled heptatonic					
	○		○					○	○	○	○
	○		○		Spanish heptatonic			○	○	○	○
	○		○		Eighttone spanish	○		Jewish malakh aobni	○	○	○
		○	Algerian		○	○		○	○	○	○
		○	Whole half diminished		○	○		○	○	Verdi enigmatic ascending	○
+50 cent ○ it bent up		○	+50 cent ○ it bent up		○ +50 cent ○ it bent up			○	○	Maqam iraqi	+50 cent ○ it bent up
		○	Whole half diminished	○		○		○	○	Verdi enigmatic ascending	○
		○	○			○		○	○	Verdi enigmatic descending	○
		○				○		○	○	○	○
		○						Blues penta cluster	○	○	○
		○			○			○	○	○	○
		○		Kourd aran Todi arobio indian	○			○	○	○	○
	○	○		○	○			○	○	○	○
	○	○		○	○	○		○	○	○	○
○	Genus chromaticum Tcherepnin nonatonic	○		Messiaen mode 3	○	Messiaen mode 3 inverse		○	○	○	
○	○	○		○	○			○	○	○	

	6 SUS 2 7 SUS 2 6 SUS 4 7 SUS 4		m 6 ø7 6 SUS 4			M 6 m 6 6 SUS 2/4		m 7 7 SUS 2/4	Mb5 6/∆7 6/∆7 SUS 2 b5	m#5 7/∆7 7/∆7 SUS 4	M 6/7/∆7 6/7/∆7 SUS 2
	M 6/7 + 7 6/7 SUS 2		7 SUS 2/4		+7 ø7 Mb5 7 m#5 7 7 SUS 4 b5 7 SUS 4 #5		M 6 6 SUS 2/4	+ ∆7	m 7/∆7 7/∆7 SUS 4	Mb5 6/7/∆7 6/7/∆7 SUS 2 b5
	M 6/7 + 7 6/7 SUS 2/4		m 7 7 SUS 2/4		+7 ø7 Mb5 7 m#5 7 7 SUS 4 #5	M 6 m 6 6 SUS 2/4	m 6/7 6/7 SUS 2/4	+ ∆7	m 7/∆7 7/∆7 SUS 4	M 6/7/∆7 6/7/∆7 SUS 2
		M 6 m 6 + ø7	m ∆7 o∆7 ∆7 SUS 2/4		o7 ø7 Mb5 6/7 6/7 SUS 4 b5	+ ∆7	m 6/7 o7 ø7 6/7 SUS 2	+ ∆7 6/∆7 SUS 4 b5 6/∆7 SUS 4 #5	M 7/∆7 7/∆7 SUS 4	M 6/7/∆7 m 6/7/∆7
		M 6 + 6 SUS 2	m ∆7 o∆7 ∆7 SUS 4	M 7/∆7 7/∆7 SUS 2/4		+7 m#5 7 7 SUS 2/4 #5		7 SUS 2	6/∆7 SUS 4	+ 7/∆7 Mb5 7/∆7 7/∆7 SUS 4 b5 7/∆7 SUS 4 #5	M 6/7/∆7 m 6/7/∆7 6/7/∆7 SUS 4
	m(1*)(3*)6/(7*) 6/7(7*) SUS 2(1*) 6/7(7*) SUS 4(1*)		m(1*) 7(7*) 7(7*) SUS 4	M(1*)(3*)6/6(*)/∆7 6/6(*)/∆7 SUS 2(1*)(5*) 6/6(*)/∆7 SUS 4(1*)(5*)	M(5*) 6/7(7*) m(5*) 6/7(7*) 6/7(7*) SUS 2(5*) 6/7(7*) SUS 4(4*)(5*) also all can be(1*)	m(3*) 7(7*) 7(7*) SUS 2	M(5*) 6/∆7 7(7*) SUS 4(4*)	ø(3*)(5*) 7/∆7 m#5(3*) 7/∆7 7/∆7 SUS 4 #5	M(1*)(5*) 6/7/∆7 6/7 SUS 2(1*)(2*) 6/7 SUS 4(1*)(4*) ∆7 SUS 2(1*)(2*) ∆7 SUS 4(4*)(4*)
		M 6 + 6 SUS 2	m ∆7 o∆7 ∆7 SUS 4	M 7/∆7 7/∆7 SUS 2/4	+7 m#5 7 7 SUS 2/4 #5		7 SUS 2	6/∆7 SUS 4	+ 7/∆7 Mb5 7/∆7 7/∆7 SUS 4 b5 7/∆7 SUS 4 #5	M 6/7/∆7 m 6/7/∆7 6/7/∆7 SUS 4
		M 6 +	m ∆7 o∆7 ∆7 SUS 4			+ m#5 6 6 SUS 2/4 #5	m 7 ø7 7 SUS 2	6/∆7 SUS 2/4 b5	+ 7/∆7 7/∆7 SUS 4 #5	M 6/7/∆7 m 6/7/∆7
		M 6 +				+ m#5 SUS 2/4 #5	ø7 7 SUS 2 b5	6/∆7 SUS 2 (no 5) 6/∆7 SUS 4 (no 5)	+ 7/∆7	m 6/7/∆7
		P5 (add 13) A5 (add 13)					o SUS 2 b5	∆7 SUS 4 (no 5)	M(no 5) 7/∆7	m(no 5) 6/7/∆7
		o7 m 6			o7 Mb5 6 6 SUS 2/4 b5		o7 6 SUS 2 b5	∆7 SUS 2/4 #5	m 7/∆7	o7 ø7 o∆7
		o7 m 6 6 SUS 2		M 7 7 SUS 4	o7/∆7 Mb5 6/∆7 6/∆7 SUS 2 b5 6/∆7 SUS 4 b5		o7 m#5 6 6 SUS 2/4 b5 6 SUS 2/4 #5	∆7 SUS 2/4	m 7/∆7	o7 ø7 o∆7 6/7/∆7 SUS 4 b5
	M 6/7 m 6/7 + 7	M 6/∆7 6/∆7 SUS 2		M 6/7 6/7 SUS 4	+∆7 o7/∆7 Mb5 6/∆7 m#5 6/∆7 6/∆7 SUS 4 b5 6/∆7 SUS 4 #5		o7 6 SUS 2/4 b5 6 SUS 2/4 #5	M ∆7 + ∆7 ∆7 SUS 2/4	M 7/∆7 m 7/∆7	o7 ø7 o∆7 6/7/∆7 SUS 2/4
	M 6/7 m 6/7 + 7 6/7 SUS 4	M 6/∆7 m 6/∆7 +∆7 o7/∆7 6/∆7 SUS 2		M 6/7 6/7 SUS 2/4	+∆7 o7/∆7 Mb5 6/∆7 m#5 6/∆7 6/∆7 SUS 4 b5 6/∆7 SUS 4 #5	M 7/∆7 m 7/∆7 + 7/∆7 7/∆7 SUS 2/4	o7 o∆7 6/7 SUS 2/4 b5 6/7 SUS 2/4 #5	M 6/∆7 + ∆7 6/∆7 SUS 2/4	M 7/∆7 m 7/∆7 + 7/∆7	m 6/7/∆7 6/7/∆7 SUS 2/4
+ SUS 2/4 b5 SUS 2/4 #5	M 6 m 6 + 6 SUS 4	M 7/∆7 m 7/∆7 +∆7 o7/∆7 7/∆7 SUS 2		+7 Mb5 6/7 6/7 SUS 2/4 b5 6/7 SUS 2/4 #5	M 6/7 m 6/7 + ∆7 6/∆7 SUS 4	M 7/∆7 m 7/∆7 +7/∆7 ø7 o∆7 7/∆7 SUS 2	+7 Mb5 6/7 6/7 SUS 2/4 b5 6/7 SUS 2/4 #5	M 6/∆7 m 6/∆7 6/∆7 SUS 4	M ∆7 m ∆7 +7/∆7 ø7 o∆7 7/∆7 SUS 2	
+7 6/7 SUS 2/4 #5	M 6/∆7 m 6/∆7 + ∆7	m 7/∆7 o7/∆7 7/∆7 SUS 2		+7 Mb5 6/7 6/7 SUS 2 b5 6/7 SUS 2 #5	M 6/∆7 m 6/∆7 6/∆7 SUS 4			+ Mb5 6 SUS 2/4 b5 6 SUS 2/4 #5	M ∆7 m ∆7 ∆7 SUS 4	M 7/∆7 m 7/∆7 ø7 o∆7 7/∆7 SUS 2	

The earth culture music rainbow

○	○	○		○	○			○	○	○	
○	○			○	Chromatic dorian inverse			○	○	○	
Symmetrical enigmatic Segiahgro	○		○		○			○	○	○	
○	○		Blues heptatonic				○	○	○	○	
○		Klara maj	○			○	○	○	○	○	
○	○					○	○	○	○	○	
○			○		○	○	○	○	○	○	
	Bebop major heptatonic		○		○	○		○	○	○	
○	○				Oriental Suban greek	○		○	○	○	
○	Bebop major octatonic		Bluse octatonic		Flaminko spanish Phrygian major	Utility minor	○		Magen abot	○	
○	+50 cent ◆ it bent up		○		○	+50 cent ◆ it bent up	○		○	Maqam esfahan	
○	○		○	○		○		○	Shosta kovich	○	
○	+50 cent ◆ it bent up		○	+50 cent ◆ it bent up		○		○	○	Maqam zangoleh	
○		○	○	○		○		○	○	Messiaen inverse 6	
○		○		○		○		○	○	○	
○		○		○	Houzam major			Neapolitan minor modes	○	○	

The earth culture music rainbow

+7 6/7 SUS 2/4 #5	M 6/△7 m 6/△7 +△7	m 7/△7 o7/△7 7/△7 SUS 2			+7 M♭5 6/7 6/7 SUS 2 ♭5 6/7 SUS 2 #5	M 6/△7 m 6/△7 6/△7 SUS 4			+ M♭5 6 SUS 2/4 ♭5 6 SUS 2/4 #5	M △7 m △7 △7 SUS 4	M 7/△7 m 7/△7 o7o△7 7/△7 SUS 2	
+7 6/7 SUS 4 #5	M 6/△7 m 6/△7 +△7				+ M♭5 6 6 SUS 4 ♭5 6 SUS 4 #5	M △7 m △7 +△7 △7 SUS 4			+ 6 SUS 2/4 #5	M △7 m △7 +△7	m 7/△7 o7o△7 7/△7 SUS 2	
m#5 6/7 6/7 SUS 4 #5	M 6/△7 +△7 6/△7 SUS 2		6/7 SUS 2/4			M 7 m 7 +7 7 SUS 4			M 6 6 SUS 2/4	M♭5 △7 m#5 △7 +△7	m 7/△7 o7o△7 7/△7 SUS 2/4	
o7 ø7 m#5 6/7	6/△7 SUS 2 6/△7 SUS 4		m 6/7 ø7 6/7 SUS 4			M 6 m 6 ø7 6 SUS 4			M 7 7 SUS 2/4	ø7 o△7 M♭5 6/△7	m#5 7/△7 7/△7 SUS 2/4 #5	
o7 ø7 6/7 SUS 2 #5		M 7 +7	m 6/△7 ø7 o△7 6/△7 SUS 4			+ ø7 M♭5 6 m#5 6 6 SUS 2 ♭5 6 SUS 2 #5			M 7 7 SUS 2	ø7 o△7 6/△7 SUS 4 ♭5	+ 7/△7 7/△7 SUS 2/4 #5	
6/7 SUS 2/4 ♭5 6/7 SUS 2/4 #5		M 7 m 7 ø7 +7				M 6 m 6 + 6 SUS 4	+ ø7 M♭5 △7 m#5 △7 △7 SUS 2 ♭5 △7 SUS 2 #5		M♭5 6/7 6/7 SUS 2 ♭5	m#5 6/△7 6/△7 SUS 4 #5	M 7/△7 + 7/△7 7/△7 SUS 2	
o7 ø7 m#5 6/7 6/7 SUS 4 ♭5 6/7 SUS 4 #5			m 6 ø7 6 SUS 2/4			M 7 m 7 7 SUS 4	ø7 o△7 M♭5 6/△7 6/△7 SUS 2 ♭5		M 6/7 6/7 SUS 2/4	ø7 o△7 m#5 6/△7	7/△7 SUS 2/4	
	M 6 +7 6 SUS 2/4		m 7 ø7 7 SUS 2/4		+7 M♭5 7 m#5 7 7 SUS 4 ♭5 7 SUS 4 #5	M 6/△7 m 6/△7 ø7 o△7 6/△7 SUS 2			6/7 SUS 2/4	+ △7 M♭5 6/△7	m 7/△7 7/△7 SUS 4	
6/7 SUS 4 ♭5 6/7 SUS 4 #5	M 6/△7 + 7/△7 6/△7 SUS 4					M m + SUS 4	M △7 m △7 o△7 △7 SUS 2		M(no 5) 6/7 6/7 SUS 2(no 5) 6/7 SUS 4(no 5)	+ △7 m#5 6/△7	m 7/△7 7/△7 SUS 2	
o7 ø7 m#5 6/7 6/7 SUS 4 ♭5 6/7 SUS 4 #5	M 6/△7 + 7/△7 6/△7 SUS 2/4		m 6/7 ø7 o7 6/7 SUS 2/4			M 7 m 7 +7 7 SUS 4	M 6/△7 m 6/△7 ø7 o△7 6/△7 SUS 2		M 6/7 6/7 SUS 2/4	ø7 o△7 M♭5 6/△7 m#5 6/△7	m 7/△7 7/△7 SUS 2/4	
o7(5*) ø7(5*) m#5 6/7 6/7 SUS 4 ♭5(5*) 6/7 SUS 4 #5	M(1*) 6/△7 +(1*) 7/△7 6/△7 SUS 2(1*) 6/△7SUS4(1*)(4*)		m(3*) 6/7 ø7(3*) ø7(3*) 6/7 SUS 2/4			M 7 m 7 +(5*) 7 7 SUS 4	M(1*)(5*) 6/△7 m(1*)(5*) 6/△7 o(1*) △7 6 SUS 2(1*)(5*) △7 SUS 2(1*)(5*)		M 6/7(7*) 6/7(7*) SUS 2 6/7(7*) SUS 4(4*)	ø7(6*) o△7 M♭5(5*) 6(6*)/△7 m#5 6(6*)/△7	m(3*) 7/△7 7/△7 SUS 2/4	
+7 o7 ø7 M♭5 6/7 m#5 6/7	m 6/△7 6/△7 SUS 2/4		m 6/7 ø7 o7 6/7 SUS 4	M♭5 6/△7 + △7 6/△7 SUS 2/4 ♭5 6/△7 SUS 2/4 #5		M 6/7 m 6/7 ø7 o7 6/7 SUS 2			M 7 + 7 7 SUS 2/4	M 6/△7 m 6/△7 o7 o△7	ø7 o△7 m#5 7/△7 7/△7 SUS 2/4 ♭5 7/△7 SUS 2/4 #5	
+(3*)7 o7 ø7 M♭5(3*)6/7 m#5 6/7	m(1*)(3*) 6/△7 6/△7SUS2/4(1*)		m 6/7(7*) ø7 ø7(7*) 6/7(7*)SUS 4	M♭5(1*) 6(6*)/△7 +(1*) △7 6(6*)/△7 SUS 4(1*) ♭5 6(6*)/△7 SUS 2(1*) ♭5		M(5*) 6(6*)/7 m(5*) 6(6*)/7 ø7(6*) ø7 6(6*)/7SUS2(5*)			M 7 +(5*)7 7 SUS 2/4(4*)	M(3*)(5*) 6/△7 m(5*) 6/△7 ø7 o△7	ø(3*)(5*)7 o(3*)(5*) △7 m#5(3*) 7/△7 7/△7SUS2/4♭5(5*) 7/△7SUS2/4#5	
+7 o7 ø7 M♭5 6/7 m#5 6/7 6/7 SUS 2 ♭5 6/7 SUS 2 #5		M 7 + 7 7 SUS 2	m 6/△7 6/△7 SUS 2	+7/△7 M♭5 7/△7 7/△7 SUS 2/4 ♭5 7/△7 SUS 2/4 #5		+7 o7 ø7 M♭5 6/7 m#5 6/7 6/7 SUS 2 ♭5 6/7 SUS 2 #5			M 7 + 7 7 SUS 2/4	m 6/△7 o7 o△7 6/△7 SUS 4	+ 7/△7 M♭5 7/△7 7/△7 SUS 2/4 ♭5 7/△7 SUS 2/4 #5	
+7 M♭5 6/7 6/7 SUS 2 ♭5 6/7 SUS 2 #5		M 7 + 7 7 SUS 2		+7 M♭5 7 7 SUS 2/4 ♭5 7 SUS 2/4 #5		+7 ø7 M♭5 7 m#5 7 7 SUS 2 ♭5 7 SUS 2 #5			+7 M♭5 7 7 SUS 2 ♭5 7 SUS 2 #5	m 6/△7 6/△7 SUS 4	+ 7/△7 M♭5 7/△7 7/△7 SUS 2 ♭5 7/△7 SUS 2 #5	
+7 6/7 SUS 2/4 #5		m 7 ø7 7 SUS 2		+7 M♭5 7 7 SUS 4 ♭5 7 SUS 4 #5	M 6/△7 m 6/△7 + △7 6/△7 SUS 2/4				+ M♭5 6 6 SUS 2 ♭5 6 SUS 2 #5	m △7 △7 SUS 4	M 7/△7 7/△7 SUS 2	

The earth culture music rainbow

					Houzam major			Neapolitan minor modes			
○		○		○	26				○	○	
○		○		○	+50 cent bent up			○	Chahargah	+50 cent bent up	
○		○		○				○	Raga viyog avara	○	
○		○		○				○	○	○	
○		○		○		○		○	○	Lydian whole tone alternate	
○		○	○	○		○		○	○	Messiaen inverse 6 (25)	
○		○	○	○		○		○	○		JG Octatonic
		○	○	○		○		○	Chromatic lydian inverse (27)		○
		○	○	Raga megh (28)		○			○		○
		○	○	○		○			○	○	○
○		○	○	○		○			○	○	○
○		○	○	○			○	○	○	○	○
Zir af kand		○	○		○		○	○	○	○	○
+50 cent bent up		Persian maqam bozorg	+50 cent bent up		+50 cent bent up		○	+50 cent bent up	○		○
○		Blues phrygian	○		Minor bebop heptatonic		○	Marvi Marva grananas raga ratment	○		
○		○			○		○	○	○		

+7 6/△7 SUS 2/4 #5		m 7 ø7 7 SUS 2		+7 M♭5 7 7 SUS 4 ♭5 7 SUS 4 #5	M 6/△7 m 6/△7 + △7 6/△7 SUS 2/4			+ M♭5 6 6 SUS 2 ♭5 6 SUS 2 #5	m △7 △7 SUS 4	M 7/△7 7/△7 SUS 2	
+7 6(6*)/△7 SUS 2 #5 6(6*)/△7 SUS 4(4*) #5		m(3*)7(7*) ø(3*) 7(7*) 7(7*) SUS 2		+7 M♭5(5*) 7 7 SUS 4 ♭5(5*) 7 SUS 4 #5	M(1*)6/△7 m(1*)6/△7 +(1*)△7 6/△7SUS2(1*) 6/△7SUS4(1*)(4*)			+ M♭5 6(6*) 6(6*)SUS2(5*)♭5 6(6*)SUS2(5*)#5	m △7 △7 SUS 4	M(1*)(5*)7/△7 7/△7SUS2(1*)(5*)	
6/7 SUS 2/4 #5		m 7 ø7			M 6 m 6 6 SUS 4			M♭5 6 6 SUS 2 ♭5	m#5 △7 △7 SUS 4 #5	M 7/△7 7/△7 SUS 2	
+7 6/7 SUS 2 #5		7 SUS 2		+7 M♭5 7 7 SUS 4 ♭5 7 SUS 4 #5				+ M♭5 SUS 2 ♭5 SUS 2 #5	m △7 △7 SUS 4	M♭5 7/△7 7/△7 SUS 2 ♭5	
+7 M♭5 6/7 6/7 SUS 2 ♭5 6/7 SUS 2 #5		M 7 + 7 7 SUS 2		+7 M♭5 7 7 SUS 2/4 ♭5 7 SUS 2/4 #5	+7 o M♭5 7 m 6/△7 7 SUS 2 ♭5 7 SUS 2 #5			+7 M♭5 7 7 SUS 2 ♭5 7 SUS 2 #5	m 6/△7 6/△7 SUS 4	+7 +△7 M♭5 7/△7 7/△7 SUS 2 ♭5	
+7 o7 o△7 M♭5 6/7 m#5 6/7 6/7 SUS 2 ♭5 6/7 SUS 2 #5		M 7 + 7 7 SUS 2	m 6/△7 o7 o△7 6/△7 SUS 4	+7/△7 M♭5 7/△7 7/△7 SUS 2/4 ♭5 7/△7 SUS 2/4 #5	+7 o7 o7 M♭5 6/7 m#5 6/7 6/7 SUS 2 ♭5 6/7 SUS 2 #5			+7 m 7 7 SUS 2	m 6/△7 o7 o△7 6/△7 SUS 4	+7 +△7 M♭5 7/△7 7/△7SUS2/4♭5	
+△7 o7 o△7 M♭5 6/△7 m#5 6/△7 6/△7 SUS 2 ♭5 6/△7 SUS 2 #5		M 6/7 + 7 6/7 SUS 2	o7 o△7 m#5 6/△7 6/△7 SUS 4 ♭5 6/△7 SUS 4 #5	M 7/△7 +7/△7 7/△7 SUS 2/4	o7 o7 m#5 6/7 6/7 SUS 2/4 ♭5 6/7 SUS 2/4 #5			M 7 m 7 +7 o7	m 6/△7 o7 o△7 6/△7 SUS 2/4		M 6/7 m 6/7 6/7 SUS 4
		M 6 6 SUS 2	o m#5 △7 △7 SUS 4 ♭5 △7 SUS 4 #5	M 7/△7 7/△7 SUS 2/4	m#5 6/7 6/7 SUS 2/4 #5			m 7	6/△7 SUS 2/4		M 6/7 m 6/7 6/7 SUS 4
		M 6 6 SUS 2	o	7/△7 SUS 2/4	m#5 6/7 6/7 SUS 2 #5				6 SUS 2/4		M 7 m 7 7 SUS 4
		M 6 6 SUS 2	o m#5 △7 △7 SUS 4 ♭5 △7 SUS 4 #5	M 7/△7 7/△7 SUS 2/4	m#5 6/7 6/7 SUS 2/4 #5			m 7	6/△7 SUS 2/4		M 6/7 m 6/7 6/7 SUS 4
+△7 o7 o△7 M♭5 6/△7 m#5 6/△7 6/△7 SUS 2 ♭5 6/△7 SUS 2 #5		M 6/7 + 7 6/7 SUS 2	o7 o△7 m#5 6/△7 6/△7 SUS 4 ♭5 6/△7 SUS 4 #5	M 7/△7 +7/△7 7/△7 SUS 2/4		o7 o7 m#5 6/7 6/7 SUS 2/4 ♭5 6/7 SUS 2/4 #5		M 7 m 7 +7 o7	m 6/△7 o7 o△7 6/△7 SUS 2/4		M 6/7 m 6/7 6/7 SUS 4
M 6/△7 m 6/△7 + △7 6/△7 SUS 2		6 SUS 2/4	+ △7 M♭5 △7 6/△7 SUS 4 ♭5 6/△7 SUS 4 #5	M 7/△7 m 7/△7 +7/△7 7/△7 SUS 4			M 6 + 6 SUS 2/4	M △7 m △7 +△7 o△7	m 7/△7 o7 o△7 7/△7 SUS 2/4		+7 m#5 6/7 6/7 SUS 4 #5
m 6/△7 6/△7 SUS 2/4		m 6/7 o7 o7 6/△7 SUS 4	+ △7 M♭5 △7 6/△7 SUS 2/4 ♭5 6/△7 SUS 2/4 #5		M 6/7 m 6/7 o7 o7 6/7 SUS 2		M 7 + 7 7 SUS 2/4	M 6/△7 m 6/△7 o7 o△7	o7 o△7 m#5 7/△7 7/△7SUS2/4♭5 7/△7SUS2/4#5		o7 o7 M♭5 6/7 m#5 6/7
m(1*)(3*)6/△7 6/△7SUS2(1*) 6/△7SUS4(1*)(4*)		m(3*)6/7(7*) o(3*)(5*)7 o(3*)(5*)7(7*)	+(1*)△7 M♭5(1*)△7 6/(7*)△7 SUS4		M(1*)6/7(7*) m(1*)6/7(7*) o(1*)(3*)7 o(1*)(3*)7(7*) 6/7(7*)SUS2(1*)		M 7(7*) +(5*)7 7(7*)SUS2/4(4*)	M(1*)(5*)6(6*)/△7 m(1*)6(6*)/△7 o(1*)7 6(6*) o(1*)△7	ø(3*)(5*)7 o(3*)(5*)7(7*)(△7*) m#5(3*)(5*)7/△(△7*)		o(5*)7(6*) ø(5*)7 M♭5(3*)6(6*)/7 m#5 6(6*)/7
m 6 6 SUS 2/4		m 7 ø7 7 SUS 2/4	M♭5 △7 6/△7SUS 2/4♭5		M 6/7 m 6/7 6/7 SUS 2		7 SUS 2	M 6/△7	o7 o△7 m#5 7/△7 7/△7 SUS 4 ♭5 7/△7 SUS 4 #5		
6 SUS 2/4		m 7 ø7 7 SUS 4			M 6 m 6 6 SUS 2		7 SUS 2	M♭5 6/△7	m#5 7/△7 7/△7 SUS 4 ♭5 7/△7 SUS 4 #5		

○		**Blues** phrygian	○		**Minor bebop** heptatonic		○	Marvi Marva grananas raga ratment	○			
○		**Blues** modified		○	○		○	○	○			
○		○		○	○			○	○			
○		○		○	Houzam major			Neapolitan minor modes	○	○		
○			**Hypo** chromatic	Persian chromatic Hipo lydian Phrygian chromatic inverse	○			○	○	○		
○			○		○			○	○	○		
	○		○		○			○	○	○		
	○	Raga todi bVL Lydian inverse Half diminished hip hop	○		○			○	○	○		
	○	Neapolitan minor	○		Mixolydian augmented		Hungarian gypsy damian emmanuel		○	○		
	○	○	○		○		○		○	○		
	○	○	Raga vijayava santa				○		○	○		
	○	Neapolitan minor	○		Mixolydian augmented		Hungarian gypsy damian emmanuel		○	○		
	○	Neapolitan Major	○		○		Lydian minor Stravinsky Raga ratipriya	Ionian arabic Major locrian				○
	○	○	○	○	○		**Raga jyoti**					○
	○	Neapolitan Major	○		○		Lydian minor Stravinsky Raga ratipriya	Ionian arabic Major locrian				○
	○	Neapolitan minor	○		Mixolydian augmented		Hungarian gypsy damian emmanuel		○	○		

6 SUS 2/4		m 7 ø7 7 SUS 4			M 6 m 6 6 SUS 2		7 SUS 2	Mb5 6/△7	m#5 7/△7 7/△7 SUS 4 b5 7/△7 SUS 4 #5		
M 6 + 6 SUS 2/4		m 7 ø7 7 SUS 2/4		+7 m#5 7 7 SUS 2 #5	M 6/△7 m 6/△7 6/△7 SUS 2		6/7 SUS 2 6/7 SUS 4	+△7 Mb5 6/△7	m 7/△7 7/△7 SUS 4		
+ 6 SUS 2/4 #5		m 7 ø7 7 SUS 2		+7 7 SUS 2 #5	M 6/△7 m 6/△7			+ Mb5 6	m △7 △7 SUS 4		
+7 6 SUS 2/4 #5 7 SUS 2/4 #5		m 7 ø7 7 SUS 2		+7 Mb5 7 7 SUS 4 b5 7 SUS 4 #5	M 6/△7 m 6/△7 o7 o△7			+ Mb5 6 6 SUS 2 b5 6 SUS 2 #5	m △7 △7 SUS 4	M 7/△7 7/△7 SUS 2	
+7 m#5 6/7 6 SUS 2/4 #5 7 SUS 2/4 #5			6 SUS 2/4	+7 +△7 m#5 7/△7 7/△7 SUS 4 b5 7/△7 SUS 4 #5	M 7/△7 m 7/△7 o7 o△7			+ M 6 6 SUS 2	m △7 o△7	7/△7 SUS 2 7/△7 SUS 4	
m#5 6/7 6 SUS 2/4 #5 7 SUS 2/4 #5			6 SUS 2/4		M 7 m 7 ø7			M 6 6 SUS 2	o△7	7/△7 SUS 2 7/△7 SUS 4	
	M 6 + 6 SUS 2		7 SUS 2/4		+7 m#5 7 7 SUS 4 #5			6 SUS 2 6 SUS 4	+△7	m 7/△7 7/△7 SUS 4	
	M 6 + 6 SUS 2	m △7 o△7	7/△7 SUS 2/4		+7 m#5 6/7 6/7 SUS 4 #5			6 SUS 2 6 SUS 4	+△7 △7 SUS 4 b5 △7 SUS 4 #5	M 7/△7 m 7/△7 7/△7 SUS 4	
	+ Mb5 6 6 SUS 2 b5 6 SUS 2 #5	m △7 △7 SUS 4	M 7/△7 7/△7 SUS 2		+7 m#5 6/7 6/7 SUS 2 #5 6/7 SUS 4 #5		m 7 ø7 7 SUS 2		+7 7 SUS 4 b5 7 SUS 4 #5	M 6/△7 m 6/△7 6/△7 SUS 4	
	+ Mb5 6 6 SUS 2 b5 6 SUS 2 #5	m △7 △7 SUS 4	M 7/△7 7/△7 SUS 2		+7 m#5 6/7 6/7 SUS 2 #5 6/7 SUS 4 #5		m 7 ø7 7 SUS 2		+7 7 SUS 4 b5 7 SUS 4 #5	M 6/△7 m 6/△7 6/△7 SUS 4	
	6 SUS 2 b5 6 SUS 2 #5	△7 SUS 4	M 7/△7				m o SUS 2		Mb5 7 7 SUS 4 b5	M(no5) 6/△7 m(no5) 6/△7 6/△7 SUS 4(no5)	
	+ Mb5 6 6 SUS 2 b5 6 SUS 2 #5	m △7 △7 SUS 4	M 7/△7 7/△7 SUS 2		+7 m#5 6/7 6/7 SUS 2 #5 6/7 SUS 4 #5		m 7 ø7 7 SUS 2		+7 7 SUS 4 b5 7 SUS 4 #5	M 6/△7 m 6/△7 6/△7 SUS 4	
	+7 Mb5 7 7 SUS 2 b5 7 SUS 2 #5	m 6/△7 6/△7 SUS 4	+7 +△7 Mb5 7/△7 7/△7 SUS 2 b5 7/△7 SUS 2 #5		+7 Mb5 6/7 6/7 SUS 2 b5 6/7 SUS 2 #5		M 7 + 7 SUS 2		+7 7 SUS 2/4 b5 7 SUS 2/4 #5		+7 o7 Mb5 7 m#5 7 7 SUS 2 b5 7 SUS 2 #5
	Mb5 7 7 SUS 2 b5	m(no5) 6/△7 6/△7 SUS 4(no5)	+7 +△7 7/△7 SUS 2 #5		6/7 SUS 2 b5 6/7 SUS 2 #5		M 7 +7				+ o Mb5 m#5 SUS 2 b5 SUS 2 #5
	+7 Mb5 7 7 SUS 2 b5 7 SUS 2 #5	m 6/△7 6/△7 SUS 4	+7 +△7 Mb5 7/△7 7/△7 SUS 2 b5 7/△7 SUS 2 #5		+7 Mb5 6/7 6/7 SUS 2 b5 6/7 SUS 2 #5		M 7 +7 7 SUS 2		+7 7 SUS 2/4 b5 7 SUS 2/4 #5		+7 o7 Mb5 7 m#5 7 7 SUS 2 b5 7 SUS 2 #5
	+ Mb5 6 6 SUS 2 b5 6 SUS 2 #5	m △7 △7 SUS 4	M 7/△7 7/△7 SUS 2		+7 m#5 6/7 6/7 SUS 2 #5 6/7 SUS 4 #5		m 7 ø7 7 SUS 2		+7 7 SUS 4 b5 7 SUS 4 #5	M 6/△7 m 6/△7 6/△7 SUS 4	

The earth culture music rainbow

	○	Neapolitan minor	○		Mixolydian augmented		Hungarian gypsy damian emmanuel		○	○
	○	Double harmonic major Raga bnari Egyptian Hungarian folk Gypsy persian	○			○	Double harmonic minor Hungarian Gypsy minor	Oriental Hizazkiar Persian	○	
	○	Chromatic hypolydian Purvi puravipvi	○			Chromatic hypodorian		○	Chromatic lydian	○
	○	Double harmonic major Raga bnari Egyptian Hungarian folk Gypsy persian	○			○	Double harmonic minor Hungarian Gypsy minor	Oriental Hizazkiar Persian	○	
	○	○	○			○	Example of pelog		○	Sabach
	Chromatic mixolydian	○	Chromatic phrygian			Chromatic dorian	○	○		○
	○	○	○			○		Blues minor Blues TB5m		Blues major
	○	○	○					Penta blues		○
	○	○	○			○		Blues minor Blues TB5m		Blues major
	Chromatic mixolydian	○	Chromatic phrygian			Chromatic dorian	○	○		○
	○	○	○			○	Example of pelog		○	Sabach
	○	○	○			○	○			○
	Oriental pentatonic uster	○	○			○	○			
	○	○	○			○	Example of pelog		○	Sabach
	○	○	○			○	○			○
	○	○	○			○	○		Oriental	○

	+ Mb5 6 6 SUS 2 b5 6 SUS 2 #5	m Δ7 Δ7 SUS 4	M 7/Δ7 7/Δ7 SUS 2		+7 m#5 6/7 6/7 SUS 2 #5 6/7 SUS 4 #5		m 7 ø7 7 SUS 2		+7 7 SUS 4 b5 7 SUS 4 #5	M 6/Δ7 m 6/Δ7 6/Δ7 SUS 4	
	6 SUS 2/4 b5 6 SUS 2/4 #5	M Δ7 +Δ7 Δ7 SUS 4	M 7/Δ7 m 7/Δ7 ø7 o7			M 6 m 6	m Δ7 Δ7 SUS 2/4		Mb5 6/7 6/7 SUS 4 b5	+Δ7 m#5 6/Δ7 6/Δ7 SUS 4 #5	
	6 SUS 2/4 6 SUS 2/4	M Δ7 +Δ7	m 7/Δ7 ø7 o7 7/Δ7 SUS 4			M 6 m 6 6 SUS 2		7 SUS 2 7 SUS 4	Mb5 6/Δ7 6/Δ7 SUS 4 b5	+7 +Δ7 m#5 7/Δ7 7/Δ7 SUS 4 #5	
	6 SUS 2/4 b5 6 SUS 2/4 #5	M Δ7 +Δ7 Δ7 SUS 4	M 7/Δ7 m 7/Δ7 ø7 o7			M 6 m 6	m Δ7 Δ7 SUS 2/4		Mb5 6/7 6/7 SUS 4 b5	+Δ7 m#5 6/Δ7 6/Δ7 SUS 4 #5	
	7 SUS 2/4 b5 7 SUS 2/4 #5	M 6/Δ7 6/Δ7 SUS 4	+7 +Δ7 ø7 o7 Mb5 7/Δ7 m#5 7/Δ7			m 6 6 SUS 4	M Δ7 +Δ7 Δ7 SUS 2		Mb5 6/7 6/7 SUS 2 b5 6/7 SUS 4 b5		M 6 m 6 + 6 SUS 2
	7 SUS 2/4 7 SUS 2/4	Mb5 6/Δ7 6/Δ7 SUS 4 b5	+7 +Δ7 m#5 7/Δ7 7/Δ7 SUS 4 #5			6 SUS 2 6 SUS 4	M Δ7 +Δ7	m 7/Δ7 ø7 o7 7/Δ7 SUS 4			M 6 m 6 + 6 SUS 2
	7 SUS 2/4 7 SUS 2/4	Mb5 6/Δ7	m#5 7/Δ7 7/Δ7 SUS 4 #5			6 SUS 2 6 SUS 4		m 7 ø7 7 SUS 4			M 6 m 6 6 SUS 2
	7 SUS 2 7 SUS 2	Diminished fifth d5 (interval) 6/Δ7	7/Δ7 SUS 4 #5					m o SUS 4			M(no5) 6 m(no5) 6 6 SUS 2(no5)
	7 SUS 2/4 7 SUS 2/4	Mb5 6/Δ7	m#5 7/Δ7 7/Δ7 SUS 4 #5			6 SUS 2 6 SUS 4		m 7 ø7 7 SUS 4			M 6 m 6 6 SUS 2
	7 SUS 2/4 7 SUS 2/4	Mb5 6/Δ7 6/Δ7 SUS 4 b5	+7 +Δ7 m#5 7/Δ7 7/Δ7 SUS 4 #5			6 SUS 2 6 SUS 4	M Δ7 +Δ7	m 7/Δ7 ø7 o7 7/Δ7 SUS 4			M 6 m 6 + 6 SUS 2
	7 SUS 2/4 b5 7 SUS 2/4 #5	M 6/Δ7 6/Δ7 SUS 4	+7 +Δ7 ø7 o7 Mb5 7/Δ7 m#5 7/Δ7			m 6 6 SUS 4	M Δ7 +Δ7 Δ7 SUS 2		Mb5 6/7 6/7 SUS 2 b5 6/7 SUS 4 b5		M 6 m 6 + 6 SUS 2
	7 SUS 2/4 b5	M(no5) 6/Δ7 6/Δ7 SUS 4(no5)	+7 +Δ7 m#5 7/Δ7			6 SUS 4	M Δ7 +Δ7				M 7 m 7 +7 7 SUS 2
	7 SUS 2/4	M(no5) Δ7 Δ7 SUS 4(no5)	M(no5) 7/Δ7 m(no5) 7/Δ7			Perfect fifth P5 Augmented fifth A5 (interval)	Perfect fifth P5 Augmented fifth A5 (interval)				
	7 SUS 2/4 b5 7 SUS 2/4 #5	M 6/Δ7 6/Δ7 SUS 4	+7 +Δ7 ø7 o7 Mb5 7/Δ7 m#5 7/Δ7			m 6 6 SUS 4	M Δ7 +Δ7 Δ7 SUS 2		Mb5 6/7 6/7 SUS 2 b5 6/7 SUS 4 b5		M 6 m 6 + 6 SUS 2
	7 SUS 2/4 b5	M(no5) 6/Δ7 6/Δ7 SUS 4(no5)	+7 +Δ7 m#5 7/Δ7			6 SUS 4	M Δ7 +Δ7				M 7 m 7 +7 7 SUS 2
	6/7 SUS 2/4 b5	+Δ7 Δ7 SUS 4 #5	M 7/Δ7 m 7/Δ7			M 6 6 SUS 2	M Δ7 m Δ7 +Δ7 o7			+ m#5 6 6 SUS 4 #5	M Δ7 m Δ7 +Δ7 Δ7 SUS 2

	O	O	O			O	O				Oriental	O
	O	O	O			Gipsy hexatonic Raga kalakanti					O	O
	O	O	O								Spanish pentatonic uster	O
	O	O	O			O						O
	Dorian tetrachord	O	O			O						
	O	O	O			O	O					
	O	O	O			O	O				O	
	O	O	O				O				O	
	O	O	Raga vijayava santa				O			O	O	
	O	O	O				O			O		
	O	O	O				Messiaen mode 4	O	Messiaen mode 4 inverse			
	O	O		O			O	O	Raga tilang			
	O	O					O	Blues #V	O			
	O	O		O			O	O	O			
	O	O		Chromatic hypodorian inverse Rock & roll			O	O	O		Greek folk Huzam	
	O	O		O			O		O		O	

	6/7 SUS 2/4 b5	+Δ7 Δ7 SUS 4 #5	M 7/Δ7 m 7/Δ7			M 6 6 SUS 2	M Δ7 m Δ7 +Δ7 oΔ7			+ m#5 6 6 SUS 4 #5	M Δ7 m Δ7 +Δ7 Δ7 SUS 2
	6/7 SUS 2 (no 5) 6/7 SUS 4 (no 5)	+Δ7	m 7/Δ7			M 6 6 SUS 4 +				+ m#5 SUS 4 #5	M Δ7 m Δ7 Δ7 SUS 2
	6/7 SUS 2 (no 5)	A5 d7 d8 (intervals)	P5 A5 A6 d8 (intervals)							M(no5) m(no5) SUS 4(no5)	M(no5) m(no5) SUS 2(no5)
	6 SUS 2 (no 5) 6 SUS 4 (no 5)	+Δ7	m 7/Δ7			M 6 +				+ m#5 SUS 4 #5	
	SUS 2 (no 5) SUS 4 (no 5)	M(no5) Δ7	m(no5) 7 m(no5) Δ7			P5 A5 d7 (intervals)					
	SUS 2 (no 5) SUS 4 (no 5)	M(no5) Δ7 Δ7 SUS 4 (no 5)	M(no5) 7/Δ7 m(no5) 7/Δ7			P5 A5 d7 (intervals)	d5 P5 A5 (intervals)				
	6 SUS 2 6 SUS 4	+Δ7 Mb5 Δ7 Δ7 SUS 4 b5 Δ7 SUS 4 #5	M 7/Δ7 m 7/Δ7 7/Δ7 SUS 4			M 6 + 6 SUS 2	m Δ7 +Δ7	7/Δ7 SUS 2 7/Δ7 SUS 4		+7 m#5 6/7 6/7 SUS 4 #5	
	6 SUS 2 b5	Δ7 SUS 4 #5	M 7/Δ7			m +				+ m#5 6 6 SUS 4 #5	
	6 SUS 2 b5 6 SUS 2 #5	Δ7 SUS 4	M 7/Δ7			m + SUS 2		Mb5 7 7 SUS 4 b5		+7 m#5 6/Δ7 6/Δ7 SUS 4 #5	
	SUS 2 b5 SUS 2 #5	Δ7 SUS 4	Mb5 7/Δ7			SUS 2		Mb5 7 7 SUS 4 b5			
	SUS 2	Δ7 SUS 4	Mb5 7/Δ7 7/Δ7 SUS 4 b5			SUS 2	Δ7 SUS 4	Mb5 7/Δ7 7/Δ7 SUS 4 b5			
	m o	Δ7 SUS 2 Δ7 SUS 4		M(no5) 6/7 m(no5) 6/7 6/7 SUS 4 (no 5)			6 SUS 2	Δ7 SUS 4 b5 Δ7 SUS 4 #5	M 7/Δ7 7/Δ7 SUS 4			
	Diminished fifth d5 Perfect fifth P5 Augmented fifth A5	Δ7 SUS 4					SUS 2	Δ7 SUS 4 b5 Δ7 SUS 4 #5	M(no5) 7/Δ7 7/Δ7 SUS 4 (no 5)			
	m o	Δ7 SUS 2 Δ7 SUS 4		M(no5) 6/7 m(no5) 6/7 6/7 SUS 4 (no 5)			6 SUS 2	Δ7 SUS 4 b5 Δ7 SUS 4 #5	M 7/Δ7 7/Δ7 SUS 4			
	m 7 o7	6/Δ7 SUS 2 6/Δ7 SUS 4		M 6/7 m 6/7 6/7 SUS 4			M 6 6 SUS 2	oΔ7 Δ7 SUS 4 b5 Δ7 SUS 4 #5	M 7/Δ7 7/Δ7 SUS 2/4			m#5 6/7 6/7 SUS 2/4 #5
	o7 m#5 7	6/Δ7 SUS 2 6/Δ7 SUS 4		m 6/7 6/7 SUS 4			M 6 6 SUS 2		M 7 7 SUS 2/4			m#5 7 7 SUS 2/4 #5

	○	○		○		○	○		○		○	
	VII Locrian half diminished Bayati	Ionian major **Bilawal** Mahur		Dorian kapl Maqam ashegh		Phrygian Arahnikzrast Bhairavi purvi Heptatonic major	Lydian Kalyan descending III to IV		Mixolydian Kamaj folk		Aeolian minor maqam nava Rast arabian Ehammedin VI Ethiopian	
	Combination shour & dashti	+50 cent ◆ it bent up		**Avaz Bayat turk**		**Avaz afshari abou ata**	○		○		○	
	Combination shour & shour	Segah +50 cent ◆ it bent up		○		○	+50 cent ◆ it bent up		○		○	
	Maqam hosseini	+50 cent ◆ it bent up		○		○	+50 cent ◆ it bent up		○		**Maqam rast**	
	Maqam rahavai	+50 cent ◆ it bent up		+50 cent ◆ it bent up		○	+50 cent ◆ it bent up		○		○	
	Maqam hijaz	+50 cent ◆ it bent up		+50 cent ◆ it bent up		○	+50 cent ◆ it bent up		+50 cent ◆ it bent up		○	
	○	○		Raga bageshri		○	○		○		○	
	Double phrygian hexatonic	○		○		○	○			○	○	
	VII Locrian half diminished Bayati	Ionian major **Bilawal** Mahur		Dorian kapl Maqam ashegh		Phrygian Arahnikzrast Bhairavi purvi Heptatonic major	Lydian Kalyan descending III to IV		Mixolydian Kamaj folk		Aeolian minor maqam nava Rast arabian Ehammedin VI Ethiopian	
	Hindi 5 bbIV Altered diminish whole tone Jewish magenabot Super locrian Melodic minor ascending	○		Javanese Bhairavi Phrygian #VI Jazz inverse Minor orvian bII	Lydian augmented Hindi #IV & #V		Overtone Mixolydian #IV Lydian dominant 7		Hindostan major minor Hendo VI&VII&V melodic minor descending bartor hindi		○	
	○	○		Combination shour & mahoor	+50 cent ◆ it bent up		○		○		○	
	Super locrian	○		**Hizaz**	○		○		○			
	○	○		○	○				**Raga zilaf**		○	
	Super locrian	○		**Hizaz**	○		○		○			
	Minor locrian half diminished	○		Javanese Bhairavi Phrygian #VI Jazz inverse Minor orvian bII	Lydian augmented Hindi #IV & #V		Overtone Mixolydian #IV Lydian dominant 7		Hindostan major minor Hendo VI&VII&V melodic minor descending bartor hindi		○	

	ø7 m#5 7	6/△7 SUS 2 6/△7 SUS 4		m 6/7 6/7 SUS 4		M 6 6 SUS 2	M 7 7 SUS 2/4		m#5 7 7 SUS 2/4 #5
	ø7 m#5 7 7 SUS 4 b5 7 SUS 4 #5	M 6/△7 6/△7 SUS 2 6/△7 SUS 4		m 6/7 6/7 SUS 2 6/7 SUS 4		m 7 7 SUS 4	M 6/△7 6/△7 SUS 2	M 6/7 6/7 SUS 2 6/7 SUS 4	m 7 7 SUS 2 7 SUS 4
	ø7 m#5 7 7 SUS 4 b5 7 SUS 4 #5	M(1*)6/△7 6/△7 SUS 2(1*) 6/△7 SUS 4(1*)		m 6/7(1*) 6/7(1*)SUS 2 6/7(1*)SUS 4		m 7 7 SUS 4	M(5*)6/△7 6/△7 SUS 2(5*)	M 6/7 6/7 SUS 2 6/7 SUS 4 (4*)	m(3*)7 7 SUS 2 7 SUS 4
	ø7 m#5 7 7 SUS 4 b5(5*) 7 SUS 4 #5	M(1*)6/△7 6/△7 SUS 2(1*) 6/△7 SUS 4(1*)		m(3*)6/7(1*) 6/7(1*)SUS 2 6/7(1*)SUS 4		m 7 7 SUS 4	M(1*)(5*)6/△7 6/△7 SUS 2(1*)(5*)	M(5*)6/7 6/7 SUS 2 (5*) 6/7 SUS 4 (4*)(5*)	m(3*)7 7 SUS 2 7 SUS 4
	ø7 m#5 7 7 SUS 4 b5(5*) 7 SUS 4 #5	M(1*)6/△7 6/△7 SUS 2(1*) 6/△7 SUS 4(1*)		m(3*)6/7(1*) 6/7(1*)SUS 2 6/7(1*)SUS 4		m 7 7 SUS 4	M(1*)(5*)6/△7 6/△7 SUS 2(1*)(5*)	M(5*)6/7 6/7 SUS 2 (5*) 6/7 SUS 4 (4*)(5*)	m(3*)7 7 SUS 2 7 SUS 4
	ø(3*)7 m#5(3*)7 7 SUS 4 b5(5*) 7 SUS 4 #5	M(1*)6/△7 6/△7 SUS 2 (1*)(2*) 6/△7 SUS 4 (1*)(4*)		m(1*)(3*)6/7(1*) 6/7(1*)SUS 2(1*) 6/7(1*)SUS 4(1*)		m 7(7*) 7(7*) SUS 4	M(1*)(5*)6(6*)/△7 6(6*)/△7 SUS 2(1*)(5*)	M(5*)6/7(1*) 6/7(1*)SUS 2(5*) 6/7(1*)SUS 4(4*)(5*)	m(3*)7 7 SUS 2 7 SUS 4(4*)
	ø(3*)(5*)7 m#5(3*)(5*)7 7 SUS 4 b5(5*) 7 SUS 4 #5(5*)	M(1*)(5*)6/△7 6/△7 SUS 2 (1*)(2*)(5*) 6/△7 SUS 4 (1*)(4*)(5*)		m(1*)(3*)6/7(1*) 6/7(1*)SUS 2(1*) 6/7(1*)SUS 4(1*)		m 7(7*) 7(7*) SUS 4	M(1*)(5*)6(6*)/△7 6(6*)/△7 SUS 2(1*)(2*)(5*)	M(1*)(5*)6/7(1*) 6/7(1*)SUS 2(1*)(5*) 6/7(1*)SUS 4(4*)(5*)	m(3*)7(7*) 7(7*) SUS 2 7(7*) SUS 4(4*)
	o m#5 SUS 4 b5 SUS 4 #5	M △7 △7 SUS 2 △7 SUS 4		m(no 5) 6/7 6/7 SUS 2(no 5) 6/7 SUS 4(no 5)		m 7	6/△7 SUS 2	M 6/7 6/7 SUS 4	
	o7 m#5 6 6 SUS 4 b5	+△7		o7 o7 6/7 SUS 2 b5		M 7 +7	m 6/△7 o7 o△7		+ o7 Mb5 6 m#5 6
	o7 m#5 7 7 SUS 4 b5 7 SUS 4 #5	M 6/△7 6/△7 SUS 2 6/△7 SUS 4		m 6/7 6/7 SUS 2 6/7 SUS 4		m 7 7 SUS 4	M 6/△7 6/△7 SUS 2	M 6/7 6/7 SUS 2 6/7 SUS 4	m 7 7 SUS 2 7 SUS 4
	+7 o7 Mb5 7 m#5 7	m 6/△7 6/△7 SUS 2 6/△7 SUS 4		m 6/7 6/7 SUS 4	+△7 Mb5 6/△7 6/△7 SUS 2 b5 6/△7 SUS 2 #5		M 6/7 6/7 SUS 2	M 7 +7 7 SUS 2 7 SUS 4	o7 m#5 7 7 SUS 2/4 b5 7 SUS 2/4 #5
	+(3*)7 o7 Mb5 7 m#5(3*)7	m(3*)6/△7 6/△7 SUS 2 6/△7 SUS 4		m 6/7 6/7 SUS 4	+(1*)△7 Mb5(1*)6/△7 6/△7 SUS 2(1*)b5 6/△7 SUS 2(1*)#5	M 6/7(7*) 6/7(7*) SUS 2		M 7 +7(7*) 7 SUS 2 7 SUS 4	ø(5*)7 m#5 7 7 SUS 2/4 b5(5*) 7 SUS 2/4 #5
	+ o Mb5 m#5	m △7 △7 SUS 2 △7 SUS 4		m(no 5) 6/7 6/7 SUS 4(no 5)	+△7 6/△7 SUS 2 #5		6/7 SUS 2	M 7 7 SUS 4	
	+ m#5	m △7 △7 SUS 2		6/7 SUS 4(no 5)	+△7 Mb5 6/△7			M SUS 4	
	+ o Mb5 m#5	m △7 △7 SUS 2 △7 SUS 4		m(no 5) 6/7 6/7 SUS 4(no 5)	+△7 6/△7 SUS 2 #5		6/7 SUS 2	M 7 7 SUS 4	
	+7 o7 Mb5 7 m#5 7	m 6/△7 6/△7 SUS 2 6/△7 SUS 4		m 6/7 6/7 SUS 4	+△7 Mb5 6/△7 6/△7 SUS 2 b5 6/△7 SUS 2 #5	M 6/7 6/7 SUS 2		M 7 7 SUS 2 7 SUS 4	ø7 m#5 7 7 SUS 2/4 b5 7 SUS 2/4 #5

	Minor locrian half diminished	○		Javanese Bhairavi Phrygian #VI Jazz inverse Minor orvian ♭II	Lydian augmented Hindi #IV & #V		Overtone Mixolydian #IV Lydian dominant 7		Hindostan major minor Hendo VI&VII&V melodic minor descending bartor hindi		○
		○	○		○	○		**Raga vutari**				○
		○	○		○	○			○			Pyramid Hexatonic
		○	Hawaiian		○	○					○	○
	Minor Locrian #2 Aeolian ♭5 Hindi ♭III & ♭V Half diminished	○			Javanese Bhairavi Phrygian #VI Jazz inverse Minor orvian ♭II	Lydian augmented Hindi #IV & #V		Overtone Mixolydian #IV Lydian dominant 7		Hindostan major minor Hendo VI&VII&V melodic minor descending bartor hindi		○
		○	Hawaiian		○	○					○	○
		○	○		○	○					○	
	Alternating tetra mirror	○			○	○						
	Minor locrian half diminished	○		Javanese Bhairavi Phrygian #VI Jazz inverse Minor orvian ♭II	Lydian augmented Hindi #IV & #V		Overtone Mixolydian #IV Lydian dominant 7		Hindostan major minor Hendo VI&VII&V melodic minor descending bartor hindi		○
	Ultra locrian	○		Pseudo turkish Locrian #VI Maj6 Locrian natural	○		○		○		**Lydian #IV**	
	○	○		○	○		○	○		Hungarian Major	
	○	○		○	○		Maqam hijaz Blues axilar Half diminished symmetrical	Axilar diminish Arabian whole half diminished			○	○
	○	○		○	○		○	○		Todi ♭V II Hindi ♭II ♭III ♭IV	○
	○			Blues dorian hexatonic	Takemitsu tree line mode		Prometheus major Neapolitan	○			○
	○	○		○	○		Romanian major Purrib VII	○			○
Harmonic major nat Bhairava Fhiopian		Dorian ♭5		○	○		○	○			○

	+7 ø7 Mb5 7 m#5 7	m 6/△7 6/△7 SUS 2 6/△7 SUS 4		m 6/7 6/7 SUS 4	+△7 Mb5 6/△7 6/△7 SUS 2 b5 6/△7 SUS 2 #5		M 6/7 6/7 SUS 2		M 7 7 SUS 2 7 SUS 4		ø7 m#5 7 7 SUS 2/4 b5 7 SUS 2/4 #5
	ø7 Mb5 7	m(no5) 6/△7 6/△7 SUS 2 (no5) 6/△7 SUS 4 (no5)		m 6/7	6/△7 SUS 2 b5 6/△7 SUS 2 #5		M 6/7				o m#5 SUS 2/4 b5 SUS 2/4 #5
	M 7 m 7	o7 o△7 6 SUS 2 b5 △7 SUS 2 b5		M 6/7	o7 o△7 m#5 6/△7			o7 m#5 6 6 SUS 4 b5 6 SUS 4 #5			o7 m#5 6 6 SUS 2/4 b5 6 SUS 2/4 #5
	+7 m#5 7	m 6/△7 6/△7 SUS 2		6/7 SUS 4	+△7 Mb5 6/△7				M + SUS 2/4		o7 m#5 6/△7 7 SUS 2/4 b5 7 SUS 2/4 #5
	+7 o7 Mb5 7 m#5 7	m 6/△7 6/△7 SUS 2 6/△7 SUS 4		m 6/7 6/7 SUS 4	+△7 Mb5 6/△7 6/△7 SUS 2 b5 6/△7 SUS 2 #5		M 6/7 6/7 SUS 2		M 7 7 SUS 2 7 SUS 4		o7 m#5 7 7 SUS 2/4 b5 7 SUS 2/4 #5
	+7 m#5 7	m 6/△7 6/△7 SUS 2		6/7 SUS 4	+△7 Mb5 6/△7				M + SUS 2/4		o7 m#5 6/△7 7 SUS 2/4 b5 7 SUS 2/4 #5
	+ m#5	m △7 △7 SUS 2		7/△7 SUS 4 (no5)	+△7				M + SUS 4		
	M(no5) m(no5)	m(no5) △7 △7 SUS 2 (no5)		A6 d7 A5 (intervals)	d8 d7 (intervals)						
	+7 o7 Mb5 7 m#5 7	m 6/△7 6/△7 SUS 2 6/△7 SUS 4		m 6/7 6/7 SUS 4	+△7 Mb5 6/△7 6/△7 SUS 2 b5 6/△7 SUS 2 #5		M 6/7 6/7 SUS 2		M 7 7 SUS 2 7 SUS 4		o7 m#5 7 7 SUS 2/4 b5 7 SUS 2/4 #5
	+ o7 Mb5 6 m#5 6	m △7 △7 SUS 2 △7 SUS 4		o7 ø7 6/7 SUS 4 b5	+△7 Mb5 6/△7 6/△7 SUS 2/4 #5		m 6/7 o7 ø7 6/7 SUS 2		M 7 + 7 7 SUS 4	M 6/△7 m 6/△7 o7 o△7	
	o7 M 6 m 6	o△7 m#5 △7 △7 SUS 2/4 b5 △7 SUS 2/4 #5		o7 ø7 Mb5 6/7	m#5 6/△7 6/△7 SUS 2/4 #5		m 6/7 o7 o7	6/△7 SUS 2/4 b5 6/△7 SUS 2/4 #5		M 6/7 m 6/7 o7 ø7		
	o7 o7 M 6/7 m 6/7	o7 o△7 m#5 6/△7 6/△7 SUS 2/4 b5 6/△7 SUS 2/4 #5		o7 ø7 M 6/7 m 6/7	o7 o△7 m#5 6/△7 6/△7 SUS 2/4 b5 6/△7 SUS 2/4 #5		M 6/7 m 6/7 o7 o7	o7 o△7 m#5 6/△7 6/△7 SUS 2/4 b5 6/△7 SUS 2/4 #5		M 6/7 m 6/7 o7 o7		o7 o△7 m#5 6/△7 6/△7 SUS 2/4 b5 6/△7 SUS 2/4 #5
	o7 o7 M 6/7 m 6/7			o7 M 6 m 6	o△7 m#5 △7 △7 SUS 2/4 b5 △7 SUS 2/4 #5		o7 o7 Mb5 6/7	m#5 6/△7 6/△7 SUS 2/4 b5		m 6/7 o7 o7		6/△7 SUS 2/4 b5 6/△7 SUS 2/4 #5
	ø7 M 7 m 7			M 6 m 6	o△7 m#5 △7 △7 SUS 2 b5 △7 SUS 2 #5		Mb5 6/7	m#5 6/△7 6/△7 SUS 4 #5				6 SUS 2/4 b5 6 SUS 2/4 #5
	o7 M 7 m 7	o7 o△7 6/△7 SUS 2/4 b5		M 6/7 m 6/7	o7 o△7 m#5 6/△7 6/△7 SUS 2 b5 6/△7 SUS 2 #5		M 6/7	o7 o△7 m#5 6/△7 6/△7 SUS 4 b5 6/△7 SUS 4 #5				o7 m#5 6 6 SUS 2/4 b5 6 SUS 2/4 #5
M △7 +△7 △7 SUS 2/4		o7 o7 6/7 SUS 2/4 b5		M 7 m 7 +7	m 6/△7 o7 o△7 6/△7 SUS 2/4		M 6/7 6/7 SUS 4	o7 o△7 +△7 6/△7 SUS 4 b5 6/△7 SUS 4 #5				o7 m#5 6 6 SUS 4 b5 6 SUS 4 #5

Harmonic major nat Bhairava Fhiopian		Dorian b5		○	○			○	○		○
○		○		○	○		Combination chaharghah & mahur	+50 cent ✦ it bent up			○
Raga paralu				○	○			○	○		○
Harmonic major nat Bhairava Fhiopian		Dorian b5		○	○			○	○		○
Raga latika		○		○			Raga Kalavati	○			○
○			○	○			Six tone symmetrical Half augmented Messiaen truncated mode 3	Augmented messiaen truncated mode			○
Raga latika		○		○			Raga Kalavati	○			○
○		○			Raga vijayanagari			○	○		○
○		○		○	○		Combination chahargah & mahur		○		○
○		○			Raga vijayanagari			○	○		○
○			○		○		Raga vasanta bnamovi	Lydian #2 hexatonic			○
○			○				Claster center Penta mirror	○			○
○			○		○		Raga vasanta bnamovi	Lydian #2 hexatonic			○
○		○	Ionian #5 Harmonic major 2		Romanian minor Dorian #4 Gnossiennes			○	○		○
○		Combination shour & chahargah	+50 cent ✦ it bent up			○		○	+50 cent ✦ it bent up		○
○		○	○				Double harmonic major Hexatonic	○			○

M △7 +△7 △7 SUS 2/4		o7 ø7 6/7 SUS 2/4 b5		M 7 m 7 +7	m 6/△7 o7 o△7 6/△7 SUS 2/4		M 6/7 6/7 SUS 4	o7 o△7 +△7 6/△7 SUS 4 b5 6/△7 SUS 4 #5		o7 m#5 6 6 SUS 4 b5 6 SUS 4 #5
M △7 +(5°)△7 △7 SUS 2/4		o(5°)7 ø(5°)7 6/7 SUS 2/4 b5(5°)		M(3°)7 m 7 +7	m(3°)6/△7 o(3°)7 o(3°)△7 6/△7 SUS 2/4		M 6/7 6/7 SUS 4	o(1°)7 o(1°)△7 +(1°)△7 6/△7 SUS 4(1°)b5 6/△7 SUS 4(1°)#5		o7 6(6°) m#5 6(6°) 6(6°) SUS 4 b5 6(6°) SUS 4 #5
M △7 +△7 △7 SUS 4				M m +	m △7 o△7 △7 SUS 2		M(no 5) 6/7 6/7 SUS 4(no 5)	+7 m#5 7		6 SUS 4 b5 6 SUS 4 #5
M △7 +△7 △7 SUS 2/4		o7 o7 6/7 SUS 2 b5 6/7 SUS 4 b5		M 7 m 7 +7	m 6/△7 o7 o△7 6/△7 SUS 2		M 6/7 6/7 SUS 4	+△7 o7 o△7 Mb5 6/7 m#5 6/△7		ø7 m#5 6 6 SUS 4 b5 6 SUS 4 #5
M △7 +△7 △7 SUS 2		6 SUS 2/4 b5 7 SUS 2/4 b5		M 7 m 7 +7			M 6 6 SUS 4	+△7 o△7 Mb5 △7 m#5 △7		m#5 6 6 SUS 4 #5
M △7 m △7 +△7			+ 6 SUS 4 #5	M △7 m △7 +△7			+ 6 SUS 4 #5	M △7 m △7 +△7		+ 6 SUS 4 #5
M △7 +△7 △7 SUS 2		6 SUS 2/4 b5 7 SUS 2/4 b5		M 7 m 7 +7			M 6 6 SUS 4	+△7 o△7 Mb5 △7 m#5 △7		m#5 6 6 SUS 4 #5
△7 SUS 2 △7 SUS 4		o7 o7 6/7 SUS 4 b5			m 6 o7 6 SUS 2		M 7 7 SUS 4	o7 o△7 Mb5 6/△7		ø7 m#5 6
M △7 +△7 △7 SUS 2/4		o7 o7 6/7 SUS 2 b5 6/7 SUS 4 b5		M 7 m 7 +7	m 6/△7 o7 o△7 6/△7 SUS 2		M 6/7 6/7 SUS 4	+△7 o7 o△7 Mb5 6/△7 m#5 6/△7		ø7 m#5 6 6 SUS 4 b5 6 SUS 4 #5
△7 SUS 2 △7 SUS 4		o7 o7 6/7 SUS 4 b5			m 6 o7 6 SUS 2		M 7 7 SUS 4	o7 o△7 Mb5 6/△7		ø7 m#5 6
m △7 △7 SUS 4			+ 6 SUS 2 #5 6 SUS 4 #5		m 7 ø7 7 SUS 2		+7 7 SUS 4 #5	M 6/△7 m 6/△7		+ Mb5 6
m △7			+ 6 SUS 4 #5				+ SUS 4 #5	M △7 m △7		+
m △7 △7 SUS 4			+ 6 SUS 2 #5 6 SUS 4 #5		m 7 ø7 7 SUS 2		+7 7 SUS 4 #5	M 6/△7 m 6/△7		+ Mb5 6
m △7 △7 SUS 2 △7 SUS 4		o7 o7 6/7 SUS 4 b5	+△7 6/△7 SUS 2/4 #5		m 6/7 o7 o7 6/7 SUS 2		M 7 +7 7 SUS 4	M 6/△7 m 6/△7 o7 o△7		Mb5 6 m#5 6
m(3°)△7 △7 SUS 2 △7 SUS 4		o(5°)7 ø(5°)7 6/7 SUS 4 b5	+(1°)△7 6/△7 SUS 4(1°#4°)#5		m(3°)6/7(1°) o(3°)7(1°) o(3°)7(1°) 6/7(1°) SUS 2		M 7 +(5°)7 7 SUS 4	M(1°)(5°)6/△7 m(1°)(5°)6/△7 o(1°) o(1°)△7		M(3°)b5 6(6°) m#5 6(6°)
m △7 △7 SUS 2		6/7 SUS 4 b5	+△7 6/△7 SUS 4 #5				M + SUS 4	M △7 m △7 o△7		Mb5 6 m#5 6

○		○	○				Double harmonic major Hexatonic	○			○	
○		Iwato	Hirajoshi Hindolita				Akebone japones Sofe descending	Chinese 2				
		○	○				Messiaen truncated mood	○				
○		Iwato	Hirajoshi Hindolita				Akebone japones Sofe descending	Chinese 2				
Raga trimurti		○	Genus secundum				Double harmonic hexatonic Miyako Bushi	○			○	
		○	○				Balish Balish felog	○			Raga kalmaji Durga	
		○	○				Kumio 2	○				○
○		Iwato	Hirajoshi Hindolita				Akebone japones Sofe descending	Chinese 2				
○		○	○					○				
		○	○					○	Messiaen truncated mode 6			
		○	○				Japones pentachord	○			○	
		○	○		○		Messiaen truncated mode 2	○			○	
		○	○				Japones pentachord	○			○	
○		○	○				Japones balinese pentachord	○				
○		○	○						○		○	
○		○	○			○			○		○	

m △7 △7 SUS 2		6/7 SUS 4 b5	+△7 6/△7 SUS 4 #5				M + SUS 4	M △7 m △7 o△7			Mb5 6 m#5 6
m SUS 2		7 SUS 4 b5	M(no 5) 6/△7 6/△7 SUS 4 (no 5)				SUS 4	M			
		SUS 4 b5	M(no 5) △7 △7 SUS 4 (no 5)				P5 A5 (intervals)	d5 P5 d8 (intervals)			
m SUS 2		7 SUS 4 b5	M(no 5) 6/△7 6/△7 SUS 4 (no 5)				SUS 4	M			
m 7 7 SUS 2		△7 SUS 4 b5 △7 SUS 4 #5	M 6/△7 6/△7 SUS 4				m SUS 4	M SUS 2		M(no 5) 6/7 6/7 SUS 2 (no 5)	
		SUS 4 b5 SUS 4 #5	M △7 △7 SUS 4				m	SUS 2		M(no 5) 6/7	
		6 SUS 4 b5	+△7 △7 SUS 4 #5				M +	m o			+ m#5 6
m SUS 2		7 SUS 4 b5	M(no 5) 6/△7 6/△7 SUS 4 (no 5)				SUS 4	M			
m#5 SUS 2 #5		Diminished fifth d5 Minor seventh m7	6/△7 SUS 4 (no 5)					M			
		Perfect fifth P5 Diminished fifth d5	6 SUS 4 b5				d5 P5 (intervals)	△7 SUS 4 b5			
		P5 d5 d7	6 SUS 4 b5 6 SUS 4 #5					m	△7 SUS 2/4 b5		M(no 5) 6/7 m(no 5) 6/7
		o7 m 6	6 SUS 2/4 b5 6 SUS 2/4 #5		o7 o△7 Mb5 6/△7			m 6	△7 SUS 2/4 b5		o7 o△7 Mb5 6/△7
		P5 d5 d7	6 SUS 4 b5 6 SUS 4 #5					m	△7 SUS 2/4 b5		M(no 5) 6/7 m(no 5) 6/7
m#5 SUS 2 #5		P5 d5 A6	6/△7 SUS 4 b5					M	o△7 △7 SUS 4 b5		
m#5 6 6 SUS 2 #5		A5 d5 A6	6/△7 SUS 4					M SUS 2		M(no 5) 7 7 SUS 2 (no 5)	
m 7 7 SUS 2		7 SUS 4 #5	M 6/△7				m SUS 4			M(no 5) 6 6 SUS 2 (no 5) 6 SUS 4 (no 5)	

The earth culture music rainbow

○		○	○				○		○	
○	**Ritsu**	○		○		Phrygian hexatonic			Philippian Scottish hexatonic	
○		○	○		○				Major pentachord	
		○	○		Oriental		○		Japanese **sakura** pentatonic	
		○	**Raga desh**		**Raga cliandra kaunskati**			**Raga shri kalyan**	Mixolydian pentatonic	
○		○	○		○			Raga yamuna kalyani Tb5 Major blues	○	
○		**Ritsu**	○		○		Phrygian hexatonic		Philippian Scottish hexatonic	
Harmonic minor Hawaiian		○	Combination mahur & dashti		○		○		○	○
New dorian hexatonic		Raga gana haravam	○		Lydian hexatonic		**Jasho major**		○	
○		Javanese Bhairavi Phrygian #VI Jazz inverse Minor orvian bII	○		○		○		○	Minor Locrian #2 Aeolian b5 Hindi bIII & bV Half diminished
Isfahan		○	○		○		Homayon	+50 cent ○ it bent up		○
○		Javanese Bhairavi Phrygian #VI Jazz inverse Minor orvian bII	○		○		○		○	Minor Locrian #2 Aeolian b5 Hindi bIII & bV Half diminished
New dorian hexatonic		Raga gana haravam	○		Lydian hexatonic		**Jasho major**		○	
Minor pentachord		○	○		○		○			
○		○	○		Mixolydian Hexatonic		○		○	
New dorian hexatonic		Raga gana haravam	○		Lydian hexatonic		**Jasho major**		○	

Col1	Col2	Col3	Col4	Col5	Col6	Col7	Col8	Col9	Col10	Col11
m 7 7 SUS 2		7 SUS 4 #5	M 6/△7			m SUS 4			M(no5) 6 6 SUS 2(no5) 6 SUS 4(no5)	
m 7 7 SUS 2 7 SUS 4		m#5 7 7 SUS 4 #5	M 6/△7 6/△7 SUS 2	6/7 SUS 2 6/7 SUS 4		m 7 7 SUS 4			M 6 6 SUS 2/4	
		m#5	△7 SUS 2	6/7 SUS 4(no5)					M SUS 4	
		m#5 SUS 4 #5	M △7 △7 SUS 2	6/7 SUS 2(no5) 6/7 SUS 4(no5)		m 7			M 6 6 SUS 4	
m 6/7 6/7 SUS 2 6/7 SUS 4		ø7 m#5 7	6/△7 SUS 2 6/△7 SUS 4	m 6/7 6/7 SUS 4			M 6 6 SUS 2		M 7 7 SUS 2/4	
m 6/7 6/7 SUS 2 6/7 SUS 4		ø7 m#5 7	6/△7 SUS 2 6/△7 SUS 4	m 6/7 6/7 SUS 4			M 6 6 SUS 2		M 7 7 SUS 2/4	
m 7 7 SUS 2 7 SUS 4		m#5 7 7 SUS 4 #5	M 6/△7 6/△7 SUS 2	6/7 SUS 2 6/7 SUS 4		m 7 7 SUS 4			M 6 6 SUS 2/4	
m 6/7 6/7 SUS 2 6/7 SUS 4		m 7 7 SUS 4	M 6/△7 6/△7 SUS 2	M 6/7 6/7 SUS 2/4		m 7 7 SUS 2/4	ø7 m#5 7 7 SUS 4 b5 7 SUS 4 #5		M 6/△7 6/△7 SUS 2/4	
m 6 6 SUS 2/4		m 7 7 SUS 4	Mb5 6/△7 6/△7 SUS 2 b5	m 6/7 6/7 SUS 2		7 SUS 2 7 SUS 4	ø7 m#5 7			
m 6/△7 6/△7 SUS 2 6/△7 SUS 4		m 6/7 6/7 SUS 4	+△7 Mb5 6/△7 6/△7 SUS 2 b5 6/△7 SUS 2 #5	M 6/7 6/7 SUS 2		M 7 +7 7 SUS 2/4	ø7 m#5 7 7 SUS 2/4 b5 7 SUS 2/4 #5			ø7 Mb5 7 m#5 7
m △7 △7 SUS 2 △7 SUS 4		o(5*)7 o(5*)7 6/7 SUS 4(4*) b5	+△7 6/△7 SUS 4(4*) #5 6/△7 SUS 2 #5	m(3*) 6/7 6/7 SUS 2		M 7 +7 7 SUS 4	M(1*) 6/△7 m(1*) 6/△7 o(1*)7 o(1*)△7			o7 6(6*) Mb5 6 m#5 6
m 6/△7 6/△7 SUS 2 6/△7 SUS 4		m 6/7 6/7 SUS 4	+△7 Mb5 6/△7 6/△7 SUS 2 b5 6/△7 SUS 2 #5	M 6/7 6/7 SUS 2		M 7 +7 7 SUS 2/4	ø7 m#5 7 7 SUS 2/4 b5 7 SUS 2/4 #5			ø7 Mb5 7 m#5 7
m 6 6 SUS 2/4		m 7 7 SUS 4	Mb5 6/△7 6/△7 SUS 2 b5	m 6/7 6/7 SUS 2		7 SUS 2 7 SUS 4	ø7 m#5 7			
m SUS 2 SUS 4		m(no5) 7 7 SUS 4(no5)	M(no5) 6/△7 6/△7 SUS 2(no5)	6/7 SUS 2		7 SUS 4				
m 7 7 SUS 2 7 SUS 4		m(no5) 6 m(no5) 7 6 SUS 4(no5) 7 SUS 4(no5)	M 6/△7 6/△7 SUS 2	6/7 SUS 2 6/7 SUS 4		m 7 7 SUS 4			M 6 6 SUS 2/4	
m 6 6 SUS 2/4		m 7 7 SUS 4	Mb5 6/△7 6/△7 SUS 2 b5	m 6/7 6/7 SUS 2		7 SUS 2 7 SUS 4	ø7 m#5 7			

New dorian hexatonic		Raga gana haravam	○		Lydian hexatonic		Jasho major		○		
		○	○		Prometheus			○		○	○
		Alternate pentatonic	○					○		○	○
		○	○		Prometheus			○		○	○
		○	○		○					○	○
		○	○		○					○	Ryukyu
○		○	○		○				Maqam bosalek	○	
Raga abhogi		Raga rukmanel Pelog 2	○		Raga valaji					○	
○		○	○			○				○	
○		○	○			○		Greek rumanikos			
Harmonic Major tetrachord		○	○			○					
○		○	○								
○		○	○			○		Greek rumanikos			
Takemitsu tree line Mode 2		○	○			Eokimo hixatonic 2			○		1&3 tones auxiliar diminish
		○	Raga nata				○		○		○
		○	○				○		○	Romanian Bacovia	

m 6 6 SUS 2/4		m 7 7 SUS 4	Mb5 6/∆7 6/∆7 SUS 2 b5		m 6/7 6/7 SUS 2		7 SUS 2 7 SUS 4		ø7 m#5 7	
		m 6 o7 6 SUS 4	+∆7 Mb5 ∆7 ∆7 SUS 2 b5		Mb5 7/∆7 7/∆7 SUS 2 b5		M 7 +7 7 SUS 2	7 SUS 2/4 b5 7 SUS 2/4 #5	ø7 Mb5 7 m#5 7	
		6 SUS 4	+∆7 Mb5 ∆7				M + SUS 2	7 SUS 2 b5 7 SUS 4 b5	M(no 5) 7 m(no 5) 7	
		m 6 o7 6 SUS 4	+∆7 Mb5 ∆7 ∆7 SUS 2 b5		Mb5 7/∆7 7/∆7 SUS 2 b5		M 7 +7 7 SUS 2	7 SUS 2/4 b5 7 SUS 2/4 #5	ø7 Mb5 7 m#5 7	
		m 6	∆7 SUS 2 b5 ∆7 SUS 2 #5		Mb5 6/7			SUS 2/4 b5 SUS 2/4 #5	ø7 Mb5 7	
		m	∆7 SUS 2		M(no 5) 6/7 6/7 SUS 4(no 5)			SUS 4 b5 SUS 4 #5	M ∆7 ∆7 SUS 4	
m(no 5) 6/7 6/7 SUS 2(no 5) 6/7 SUS 4(no 5)		m 7	6/∆7 SUS 2		M 6/7 6/7 SUS 4			o m#5 SUS 4 b5 SUS 4 #5	M ∆7 ∆7 SUS 2 ∆7 SUS 4	
m(no 5) 6 6 SUS 2(no 5) 6 SUS 4(no 5)		m 7	6/∆7 SUS 2 b5		M 6/7			o m#5 SUS 4 b5 SUS 4 #5		
o7 6 SUS 2 b5		M 7	o7 o∆7			o7		o7 SUS 4 b5		
o m#5 SUS 2 b5 SUS 2 #5		Mb5 7	m(no 5) 6/∆7 6/∆7 SUS 4(no 5)			6 SUS 2/4 b5 6 SUS 2/4 #5	M 7 +7			
o		M(no 5) 7	m(no 5) 6/∆7			Diminished fifth d5 Augmented fifth A5				
m(no 5) Minor third m3		Minor seventh m7 interval	Major sixth M6 Minor seventh m7							
o m#5 SUS 2 b5 SUS 2 #5		Mb5 7	m(no 5) 6/∆7 6/∆7 SUS 4(no 5)			6 SUS 2/4 b5 6 SUS 2/4 #5	M 7 +7			
ø7 m#5 7 7 SUS 2 b5 7 SUS 2 #5		+7 Mb5 7	m 6/∆7 6/∆7 SUS 4			+ Mb5 6 6 SUS 2 b5 6 SUS 2 #5		M 7 +7 7 SUS 2		+7 7 SUS 2/4 #5	
		+ Mb5	m ∆7 ∆7 SUS 4			+ 6 SUS 2 #5		7 SUS 2		+7 7 SUS 4 #5	
		M +	m ∆7 o∆7			+ m#5 6			SUS 4 b5	+ SUS 4 #5	

The earth culture music rainbow

		○	○			○			○	Romanian Bacovia	
		Scriabin	○			○			○		○
		Insen Kokin joshi soft ascended tapon	○				○		○		○
Dorian pentatonic Kumoi japan			○	○			**Han kumo**		Raga tayakauns Kokinchoshi		
○		○	Major 6 add maj7			Pyomy			○		
		○	**Major maj 7**			○			○		
○		○	Major 6 add maj7			Pyomy			○		
○		○	○					Japonys 2 laydian penta chord	○		
Warao tetrachord		○	○							**Major ionian** tetrachord	
○		○	○		○					Major pentachord	
Raga abhogi	Raga rukmanel Pelog 2	○		**Raga valaji**					○		
○		○		○					○		
Minor add 6 th			**Kung**		Dominant pentatonic		○		**Minor** add 6 th		
○			○		○		○				
Minor #5 sus 2 #5				○		**Minor 7** Messiaen truncated mode			**Major 6**		
○			○			○			**Major 7**		

		M +	m Δ7 oΔ7			+ m#5 6			SUS 4 b5	+ SUS 4 #5	
		M 6	oΔ7			m#5 6 6 SUS 4 #5			6 SUS 2/4 b5		M 7 m 7
		6 SUS 4	+Δ7			M SUS 2 M (add 9)			SUS 2/4 b5		+7 m#5 7
m 6 6 SUS 2		SUS 4	Mb5 6/Δ7				SUS 2/4		ø7 7 SUS 4 b5		
m 7 7 SUS 2		7 SUS 4 #5	M 6/Δ7				m SUS 4			M(no5) 6 6 SUS 2(no5) 6 SUS 4(no5)	
		SUS 4 #5	M Δ7				m			M(no5) 6 6 SUS 4(no5)	
m 7 7 SUS 2		7 SUS 4 #5	M 6/Δ7				m SUS 4			M(no5) 6 6 SUS 2(no5) 6 SUS 4(no5)	
m#5 7 7 SUS 2 #5		Diminished fifth d5 ø7 (no3)	6/Δ7 SUS 4					M		M(no5) 7 7 SUS 2(no5) 7 SUS 4(no5)	
m(no5) 7 7 SUS 2(no5)		Augmented fifth A5 +7 (no3)	Perfect fifth P5 6/Δ7 (no3)							M(no5) SUS 2(no5) SUS 4(no5)	
m(no5) 7 7 SUS 2(no5) 7 SUS 4(no5)		m#5 7	6/Δ7 SUS 2		6/7 SUS 4					M SUS 2/4	
m(no5) 6 6 SUS 2(no5) 6 SUS 4(no5)		m 7	6 SUS 2 b5 Δ7 SUS 2 b5		M 6/7				o m#5 SUS 4 b5 SUS 4 #5		
m(no5) 6 6 SUS 4(no5)			6 SUS 2 b5		M 7				o m#5		
m 6 6 SUS 4			Mb5 6 6 SUS 2 b5		M 7 7 SUS 2		7 SUS 2 #5 7 SUS 4 #5		ø7 m#5 7		
m SUS 4 m (add 11)			M(no5) 6 6 SUS 2(no5)		7 SUS 2		7 SUS 4 #5				
m#5 SUS 4 #5			6 SUS 2(no5) 6 SUS 4(no5)		m 7			M 6			
o			m(no5) 6 6 SUS 4(no5)			6 SUS 2 b5		M 7			

○			○			○		Major 7		
○		○				Messiaen truncated mode		○		
○		○		○		○		○		
		Kung		Dominant pentatonic		○		○		Minor add 6 th
		Whole tone tetramirror		○		○		○		
	○			○		○		○		
	Minor pentatonic Bunshiki choja hard japones			Pentatonic major Mongolians Chinese		Suspended Egyptian Natural pentatonic		Minor pentatonic Raga harikauns malkauns		Example slondro Chinese yo
	○			Blues hexatonic major		○	○	Blues hexatonic minor		○
	Minor pentatonic Bunshiki choja hard japones			Pentatonic major Mongolians Chinese		Suspended Egyptian Natural pentatonic		Minor pentatonic Raga harikauns malkauns		Example slondro Chinese yo
	Major suspended 4th chord					Eskimo tetratonic		○		○
	Sus 4					○		○		
	○					○				Sus 2
		○				○				Minor triad
			○			○				Major triad
			○				○			Augmented triad
		○				○				Minor triad

o			m(no5) 6 6 SUS 4(no5)			6 SUS 2 b5		M 7			
	SUS 2 b5 SUS 2 #5	Mb5 7				SUS 2 b5 SUS 2 #5		Mb5 7			
	+ SUS 2 b5 SUS 2 #5	Mb5 7 7 SUS 2 b5		+7 SUS 2 #5		7 SUS 2 b5 7 SUS 2 #5		+7 7 SUS 4 #5			
		Mb5 6 6 SUS 2 b5		M 7 7 SUS 2		7 SUS 2/4 #5		ø7			m 6 6 SUS 4
		Mb5 SUS 2 b5		M(no5) 7 7 SUS 2(no5)		7 SUS 2 #5		Diminished fifth d5 ø7(no5)			
	m SUS 4 m (add 11)			M(no5) 6 6 SUS 2(no5)		7 SUS 2		7 SUS 4 #5			
	m 7 7 SUS 4			M 6 6 SUS 2		7 SUS 2/4		m#5 7 7 SUS 4 #5			6 SUS 2/4
	m 7 ø7 7 SUS 4			M 6 m 6 6 SUS 2		7 SUS 2/4	Mb5 6/△7	m#5 SUS 4 #5			6 SUS 2/4
	m 7 7 SUS 4			M 6 6 SUS 2		7 SUS 2/4		m#5 7 7 SUS 4 #5			6 SUS 2/4
	7 SUS 4					SUS 2/4		m(no5) 7 7 SUS 4(no5)			6 SUS 2
	SUS 4					SUS 2		7 SUS 4(no5)			
	7 SUS 4(no5)					SUS 4					SUS 2
		M(no5) 6				SUS 4 #5					m
			m#5			6 SUS 4(no5)					M
			+			+					+
		M(no5) 6				SUS 4 #5					m

		○				○					**Minor triad**
		○			○						Diminished triad
											Perfect unison P1 Diminished second d2
										○	Minor second m2 Augmented unison A1
									○		Major second M2 Diminished third d3
								○			Minor third m3 Augmented second A2
							○				Major third M3 Diminished fourth d4
						○					Perfect fourth P4 Augmented third A3
					○						Diminished fifth d5 Augmented fourth A4
				○							Perfect fifth P5 Diminished sixth d6
			○								Minor sixth m6 Augmented fifth A5
		○									Major sixth M6 Diminished seventh d7
	○										Minor seventh m7 Augmented sixth A6
○											Major seventh M7 Diminished octave d8

		M(no5) 6					SUS 4 #5						m
		m(no5) 6			Diminished fifth d5								o
Perfect unison P1 Diminished second d2													
Minor second m2 Augmented unison A1	○												
Major second M2 Diminished third d3		○											
Minor third m3 Augmented second A2			○										
Major third M3 Diminished fourth d4				○									
Perfect fourth P4 Augmented third A3					○								
Diminished fifth d5 Augmented fourth A4						○							
Perfect fifth P5 Diminished sixth d6							○						
Minor sixth m6 Augmented fifth A5								○					
Major sixth M6 Diminished seventh d7									○				
Minor seventh m7 Augmented sixth A6										○			
Major seventh M7 Diminished octave d8											○		

www.ingramcontent.com/pod-product-compliance
Lightning Source LLC
Chambersburg PA
CBHW080551230426
43663CB00015B/2793